KIDS STUFF
CHINESE

KIDS STUFF CHINESE

Easy Chinese Phrases for You and Your Kids

全 家 学 简 单 中 国 话

Therese Slevin Pirz

Translation by Chang-Nan Chen

BILINGUAL KIDS SERIES

CHOU CHOU PRESS
4 Whimbrel Court
Bluffton SC 29909
www.Chouchou@Hargray.com

Printed in the United States of America

First Edition.

ISBN   978-0-9789152-1-6

Cataloging-in-Publication Data

Pirz, Therese Slevin.

Kids stuff Chinese : Easy Chinese phrases for you and your kids by Therese Slevin Pirz ; translated by Chang-Nan Chen.
Chou Chou Press, 2008.
187 p. : illus. ; cm. -- (Bilingual Kids)
ISBN   978-0-9789152-1-6

Description: A collection of easy, child-centered phrases arranged by activity and rendered in Chinese. Pinyin is given for the Chinese sentences. Index.

1. Chinese language--Conversation and phrase books--English.
2. Chinese language--Textbooks for foreign speakers--English.
3. Chinese language--Study and teaching--English.
4. Home schooling.

I.   Title. II. Title: Easy Chinese phrases for you and your kids. III. Series: Bilingual kids
                                                        495.1–dc22

Order direct from the publisher:

Chou Chou Press
4 Whimbrel Court
Bluffton, SC 29909
www.Bilingualkids.com

Thy Kingdom come,
wáng-guó jiàng-lín
王　国　降　临,

Thy will be done on earth as it is in Heaven.
zài rén-jiān rú-tóng zài tiān-táng
在 人 间　如 同 在 天　堂.

CONTENTS
ACKNOWLEDGMENTS
PREFACE

7

VOCABULARY

Child's name:_____

Animal year of birth (rabbit, horse, dragon, etc.):_____

Received this book from:_____

Occasion:_____Date:_____

First indication of child's understanding Chinese:_____

_____

Child's first word in Chinese:_____

Child's favorite Chinese word:_____

Favorite Chinese books or stories:_____

_____

_____

Favorite Chinese videos, DVD's or CD's:_____

_____

Favorite things to do in Chinese:_____

_____

Favorite Chinese foods:_____

_____

Favorite Chinese games to play:_____

_____

ACKNOWLEDGMENTS

My hearty thanks go to Nan Chen for all her fine work in translating <u>Kids Stuff Chinese</u>. Nan has done a thorough, conscientious and professional job playing a role far and away more influential than that of translator only. Her concern for the quality of the text and her pride in presenting her native language for others to learn are admirable. The entire process has been a labor of love.

I would also like to thank Rose Hawkins from the North Shore Public Library in Shoreham, NY for getting this project started by introducing Nan Chen to the Bilingualkids family.

A grateful acknowledgement, too, to all those supporters – parents, teachers, and librarians – who see the need for learning foreign languages in this world of ours, and are doing something about it. Thank you for your wisdom.

Finally, to my husband a big "Thank you" for being supportive and steadfast through all the decision-making and uncertainties that exist during the course of bringing a book like this to publication. Joe has been a steadying influence, and has brought much enjoyment and satisfaction to the project.

PREFACE

This book covers the range of children's interests from infancy to teens. It is meant to cover not so much the calendar age of children but rather their activities and interests regardless of what birthdays they have passed. This perspective has been taken because children develop at different rates, and it is hard to predict where they will be and what their experiences will be at any particular age.

The author has researched many books in preparation for the Kids Stuff Series, and has found the Kids Stuff Series to be unique because it translates phrases and sentences which are directed to children. Because of this perspective, the Kids Stuff Series enables the user to speak to children, to carry on a conversation with children, and to model sentences that children can use naturally and readily.

At whatever age you begin your foreign language adventure, you will find this book an invaluable source for your journey. Good luck with this adventure. Make it fun! (The longest chapters are "Fun" and "Saturday Afternoon"!)

It's on the tip of my tongue. jiù zài wǒ de shé jiān er shàng

就 在 我 的 舌 尖 儿 上

Greetings

wèn hòu 问候

Start your day with this chapter. Saying your first words in Chinese will help you build momentum to continue the rest of the day in Chinese. Chinese is such a lively language. Hearing it will make you feel cheerful when spoken by you or by your child.

Hello! nǐ hǎo 你好!

Good morning!	How are you?	It's you!
zǎo	nǐ hǎo!	shì nǐ yà
早!	你 好?	是 你 呀!

How do you <u>feel</u>?
<u>gǎn-jué</u> **zěn-me** yàng
感 觉 怎 么 样?

I'm all right.
wǒ méi shì-er
我 没 事 儿。
shì-er = matter

Give me a <u>hug</u>.
<u>bào-bào</u> wǒ
抱 抱 我。

Give me a <u>kiss</u>.
<u>qīn-qīn</u> wǒ
亲 亲 我。

Hello!
wèi
喂！

-Answering the telephone - Hello! Who's speaking?
wèi, nǎ wèi
喂, 哪 位？

Speaking! This is.....speaking.
wǒ shì······
我 是

I'm **looking** to speak to…
wǒ **zhǎo**……
我 找……

It <u>is</u> *only* I.(Polite)
(Person receiving call)

It's *only* me.(Slang)
wǒ *jiù* shì
我 就 是。

I'll *call* you back/ **again**/.
wǒ **zài** *dǎ* gěi nǐ
我 再 打 给 你。

Call...(sb on the **phone**)
dǎ **diàn-huà**
打 电 话。

Goodbye.
zài-jiàn
再 见。

<u>I wish</u> you good **luck**.
<u>zhù</u> nǐ hǎo **yùn**
祝 你 好 运。

Good/ **afternoon**/ <u>evening</u>/.
xià-wǔ hǎo/ <u>wǎn-shàng</u> hǎo
下 午 好/ 晚 上 好。

14

Good night.
wǎn-ān
晚 安。

/See you/ Until/ *tomorrow*!
míng-tiān **jiàn**
明 天 见!

See you in the *afternoon*.
xià-wǔ **jiàn**
下 午 见。

See you <u>tomorrow</u> *afternoon*.
<u>míng-tiān</u> *xià-wǔ* **jiàn**
明 天 下 午 见。

See you in the <u>evening</u>.
<u>wǎn-shàng</u> **jiàn**
晚 上 见。

Come in! **Enter!**
qǐng jǐn
请 进!

I'm **glad** to <u>see</u> you.
hěn **gāo-xìng** <u>jiàn</u> dào nǐ
很 高 兴 见 到 你。

It's *really* good to <u>see</u> you!
<u>jiàn</u> dào nǐ *zhēn* hǎo
见 到 你 真 好!

How are you?
nǐ hǎo ma
你 好 吗?

(Very) well, **thanks**.
hén hǎo, **xiè-xie**
很 好, 谢谢。

<u>Long time</u> no **see**!
<u>hǎo jiǔ</u> bú **jiàn**
好 久 不 见!

Is (*a person*) around?
_____ zài ma
_____ 在 吗?

Please *speak* more <u>slowly</u>.
qǐng *shuō* <u>màn</u> yì-diǎn
请 说 慢 一点.

15

Get <u>well</u> **soon.**
kuài-kuài <u>hǎo-qǐ-lái</u>
快　快　好　起来。

And you?
nǐ nā
你 呢?

What's new?
zuì-jìn zěn-me-yàng
最　近　怎　么　样?
zuì-jìn= recently; zěn-me-yàng = how

Nothing new (with me).
lǎo yang-zi
老　样　子。

I *will* **miss** you.
wǒ *huì* **xiǎng** nǐ de
我　会　想　你　的。

Did you **miss** me?
nǐ **xiǎng** wǒ lē ma
你　想　我　了　吗?

<u>What</u> did you **bring** me?
nǐ gěi wǒ **dài** <u>shén-me</u> lē
你　给　我　带　什　么　了?

What **can** I *do* <u>for</u> you?
wǒ **néng** <u>wèi</u> nǐ *zuò* shén-me
我　能　为　你　做　什　么?

Do you *need* any **help?**
xū-yào **bāng-máng** ma
需　要　帮　忙　吗?

Not **so** good. Not **so** well.
bú **tài** hǎo
不　太　好。

So-so.
mǎ mǎ hū hū
马　马　虎　虎。
mǎ = horse; hū = tiger

See you later. So long.
huí-**jiàn**
回　见.

16

See you *again*!
*zài-***jiàn**
再 见!

Have/ a good time/ fun/!
hǎo hāo wán-er
好 好 玩 儿!

Safe and peaceful journey!
yí-lù **píng-ān**
一 路 平 安!

Send regards to…Say hello to…
tì wǒ wèn-hǎo
替 我 问 好。

wèn = ask

Excuse me.
láo-jià/ duì-bù-qǐ
劳 驾 / 对 不 起。

I beg your pardon? Say it again.
zài shuō yí biàn
再 说 一 遍。

Thank **God**!
gǎn-xiè **shàng-dì**
感 谢 上 帝!

God bless you! Bless you!
shàng-dì bǎo-yòu nǐ
上 帝 保 佑 你!

Congratulations!
zhù-hè nǐ
祝 贺 你!

To your health!
zhù nǐ **jiàn-kāng**
祝 你 健 康!

zhù nǐ = I wish you

Happy **Birthday**!
shēng-rì *kuài-lè*
生 日 快 乐!

Merry Christmas!
shèng-dàn *kuài-lè*
圣 诞 快 乐!

Happy **New** Year!
xīn-nián *kuài-lè*
新 年 快 乐!

17

Please.   **Thank you.**   You're welcome.
qǐng / qǐng nǐ...   xiè-xiè   bú xiè
请。 请 你...   谢 谢。   不 谢.

Thank you for *all* you <u>do</u>.   Welcome!   **Nice** to meet you.
xiè-xiè **nǐ** <u>zuò</u> de *yí-qiè*   huān-yíng   hěn **gāo-xìng** rèn-shi nǐ
谢 谢 你 做 的 一 切.   欢 迎!   很 高 兴 认 识 你。

Do you *speak* **English**? <u>How</u> do you **say**...? I (don't) *speak* **English**.
nǐ *shuō* **yīng-yǔ** ma   zěn-me **shuō** ...   wǒ (bù) *shuō* **yīng-yǔ**
你 说 英 语 吗?   怎 么 说...?   我 (不) 说 英 语。

What is your **name**?   My name is ...   *Where* do you **live**?
nǐ jiào *shén-me* **míng-zì**   wǒ jiào...   nǐ **zhù** zài *nǎ-lǐ*
你 叫 什 么 名 字?   我 叫......   你 住 在 哪 里?

I <u>must</u> be off now.   Take care.   The same to you.
wò **gāi** zǒu le   màn zǒu   nǐ yě shì
我 该 走 了。   慢 走。   你 也 是。

màn = slowly; zǒu = walk

O.K? All right?
xíng ma
行 吗?

18

From head to toe   cóng tóu dào jiǎo

从 头 到 脚

Bathroom   cè suǒ 厕所/yù shì 浴室

Every family member knows how much time is spent in the bathroom showering, bathing, singing, soaking, admiring.... A good time to practice your Chinese looking in the mirror or aloud in the shower.

Today will be a good day. jīn-tiān jiāng shì yí-gè hǎo tiān

今 天 将 是 一 个 好 天。

Do you need <u>to go to</u> the **bathroom**?

nǐ yào <u>qù</u> **cè-suǒ** ma

你 要 去 厕 所 吗?

Tell me when you need <u>to go to</u> the **bathroom**.

nǐ yào shì xiǎng <u>qù</u> **cè-suǒ** jiù *gào-sù* wǒ

你 要 是 想 去 厕 所 就 告 诉 我。

Bathroom _____ cè suǒ 厕所/yù shì 浴室

Go <u>get washed</u>.
qù <u>xǐ-yì-xǐ</u>
去 洗 一 洗。

Your face is/ *dirty*/ <u>clean</u>/.
nǐ-de liǎn hěn/ *zāng*/ <u>gān-jìng</u>/
你 的 脸 很/ 脏/ 干 净。

Wash your **face** and <u>hands</u>.
xǐ **liǎn** *xǐ* <u>shǒu</u>
洗 脸 洗 手。

You did <u>not</u> *wash* your **face**.
nǐ <u>méi-yǒu</u> *xǐ* **liǎn**
你 没 有 洗 脸。

Don't <u>forget</u> to *wash* your **face**.
<u>bié</u> wàng le *xǐ* **liǎn**
别 忘 了 洗 脸。

Did you *wash* your **neck**?
xǐ **bó-zi** le ma
洗 脖 子 了 吗?

Don't *bite* your <u>fingernails</u>.
bié *yǎo* <u>zhǐ-jiā</u>
别 咬 指 甲。

Clean your <u>fingernails</u>.
bǎ <u>zhǐ-jiā</u> *xǐ* **gān-jìng**
把 指 甲 洗 干 净。

Your **toothbrush** is <u>on</u> the *sink*.
nǐ-de **yá-shuā** <u>zài</u> *shuǐ-chí* shàng
你 的 牙 刷 在 水 池 上。

Brush your <u>teeth</u>.
shuā <u>yá</u>
刷 牙。

Wash **behind** your <u>ears</u>.
xǐ <u>ěr-duō</u> **hòu-biān**
洗 耳 朵 后 边。

Turn on the <u>water faucet</u>.
kāi <u>shuǐ-lóng-tóu</u>
开 水 龙 头。

Turn off the <u>water faucet</u>.
guān <u>shuǐ-lóng-tóu</u>
关 水 龙 头。

Are you having a **bath**?
nǐ zài **xǐ-zǎo** ma
你 在 洗 澡 吗?

I'm <u>running</u> a **bath** for you.
wǒ <u>fàng-shuǐ</u> gěi nǐ **xǐ-zǎo**
我 放 水 给 你 洗澡。

Look and see the <u>water</u> *run*?
kàn-jiàn <u>shuǐ</u> zài *liú* ma
看 见 水 在 流 吗?

The water is/ too **hot**/ too *cold*/ <u>just right</u>/.
shuǐ/ tài **rè** / tài *liáng*/ <u>zhèng-hǎo</u>
水/ 太 热/ 太 凉 / 正 好。

That's **enough** <u>water</u>.
<u>shuǐ</u> **gòu** le
水 够 了。

You need *a little* **more** <u>soap</u>.
duō cā *diǎn-er* <u>féi-zào</u>
多 擦 点 儿 肥皂。

I'm **washing** your *back*, <u>knees</u>, toes.
wǒ bāng nǐ **xǐ** *hòu-bèi*, <u>xī-gài</u>, jiǎo-zhǐ
我 帮 你 洗 后背, 膝盖, 脚 趾。

The soap **smells good**, *but* it is very <u>slippery</u>.
féi-zào hěn **xiāng**, *dàn-shì* hěn <u>huá</u>
肥皂 很 香, 但 是 很 滑。

Don't *use* <u>so</u> <u>much</u> soap.
bié *yòng* **zhè-me** <u>duō</u> féi-zào
别 用 这 麽 多 肥皂。

<u>Dry</u> yourself well.
bǎ shēn shàng quán <u>cā gān</u>
把 身 上 全 擦 干。
quán = all, complete

<u>Empty</u> the bath **tub**.
bǎ **zǎo-pén** lǐ de <u>shuǐ fàng diào</u>
把 澡 盆 里 的 水 放 掉。
diào = drop, out

Fold the <u>towel</u>.
bǎ <u>máo-jīn</u> **dié** hǎo
把 毛 巾 迭 好。

Bathroom _____ cè suǒ 厕所/yù shì 浴室

Hang up the **face cloth**.
bǎ **xǐ-liǎn-jīn** guà hǎo
把 洗 脸 巾 挂 好。

Is the **light** off?
guān **dēng** le ma.
关 灯 了 吗?

Do you **like** to *take a bath*?
nǐ **xǐ-huān** *xǐ-zǎo* ma
你 喜 欢 洗 澡 吗?

Yes. I **like** it.
xǐ-huān
喜 欢。

No. I don't **like** it.
bù **xǐ-huān**
不 喜 欢。

You **look** good.
nǐ **kàn** qǐ lái hěn hǎo
你 看 起 来 很 好。

Today **will be** a good day!
Jīn-tiān **jiāng shì** yí-gè hǎo tiān
今 天 将 是 一 个 好 天!

It fits like a glove.

zhèng hé shì
正 合 适.

Getting Dressed

chuān yī-fú 穿衣服

Is it to be the action-figure outfit or the cowboy outfit this morning? When you are in a hurry these are not options. Perhaps, instead, when your little girl dresses her doll, or your little guy is playing with his action figures, you and they can try some of these phrases.

What shall I wear today? wǒ jīn-tiān gāi chuān shén-me yī-fú
我 今 天 该 穿 什 么 衣 服?

Get up! It's *time* to <u>get up</u>!
qǐ-lái! *gāi* <u>qǐ-chuáng</u> le
起 来! 该 起 床 了!
chuáng_=bed

I'm **changing** your <u>diaper</u>.
wǒ gěi nǐ **huàn** <u>niào-bù</u>
我 给 你 换 尿 布。

Put your **hand** *through* the <u>sleeve</u>.
bǎ **shǒu** *chuān guò* <u>xiù-zì</u>
把 手 穿 过 袖 子。

23

Put your **foot** in the <u>shoe</u>.
bǎ **jiǎo** *fàng* jìn <u>xié</u> lǐ
把 脚 放 进 鞋 里。

You have *put* your **foot** into the **wrong** <u>shoe</u>.
nǐ-de **jiǎo** *chuān* **cuò** <u>xié</u> le
你 的 脚 穿 错 鞋 了。

What (<u>clothes</u>) will you *wear*?
nǐ *chuān* nǎ jiàn <u>yī-fú</u>
你 穿 哪 件 衣 服?
jiàn – measure word for clothing

Button your shirt.
jì shàng <u>yī-fú</u> **kòu-zi**
系 上 衣 服 扣 子。
jì shàng = buckle

Where is your **hat**?
nǐ-de **mào-zi** *nā*
你 的 帽 子 呢?

I can't find it.
wo zhǎo bù zháo
我 找 不 着。

<u>Zip up</u> your **jacket**.
bǎ **wài-tào** <u>lā-liàn lā-shàng</u>
把 外 套 拉 链 拉 上。

<u>Un-zip</u> your **jacket**.
bǎ **wài-tào** <u>lā-liàn lā-xià-lái</u>
把 外 套 拉 链 拉 下 来。

<u>Look for</u> your **gloves**.
bǎ **shǒu-tào** <u>zhǎo</u> chū-lái
把 手 套 找 出 来。
chū-lái = come out

Dress *yourself*. (<u>clothes</u>)
zì-jǐ **chuān** <u>yī-fú</u>
自 己 穿 衣 服。

24

Can you **dress** <u>yourself</u>?
nǐ *néng* <u>zì-jǐ</u> **chuān yī-fú** ma
你 能 自 己 穿 衣 服 吗?

Put on your <u>underwear</u>.
chuān-shàng <u>nèi-yī</u>
穿 上 内 衣。

Wear your <u>new</u> *coat*.
chuān nǐ-de <u>xīn</u> *wài-tào*
穿 你 的 新 外 套。

Let me **help** you *tie* your <u>shoelace</u>.
wǒ **bāng** nǐ *jì* <u>xié-dài-er</u>
我 帮 你 系 鞋 带 儿。

There's a *knot* in your <u>shoelace</u>.
nǐ-de <u>xié-dài-er</u> dǎ *jié* le
你 的 鞋 带 儿 打 结 了。

/**Comb**/ **Brush**/ your <u>hair</u>.
shū <u>tóu-fà</u>
梳 头 发。

Here are your **brush** and <u>comb</u>.
nǐ-de fà **shuā** hé <u>shū-zi</u> zài *zhè-lǐ*
你 的 发 刷 和 梳 子 在 这 里。

How <u>nice (pretty, beautiful)</u> you **look**!
nǐ **kàn qǐ-lái** hěn <u>piào-liàng</u>
你 看 起 来 很 漂 亮!

What (**clothes**) shall I <u>wear</u> *today*?
wǒ *jīn-tiān* gāi <u>chuān</u> shén-me **yī-fú**
我 今 天 该 穿 什 么 衣 服?

gāi = should; chuān = wear (clothes)

Early bird catches the worm   zǎo qǐ de niǎo yǒu chóng chī
早 起 的 鸟 有 虫 吃

Mealtime   chī fàn shí jiān 吃饭时间

Meals are a wonderful time to talk about your activities in Chinese.
You'll cement your vocabulary and expressions in a repetitive, and
amusing fashion. Spice up your sentences with words listed in the
vocabulary at the back of this book.

Enjoy your meal!   hǎo hāo chī fàn   好好吃饭!

Do you **want** <u>to eat</u> *breakfast*?
xiǎng <u>chī</u> *zǎo-fàn* ma
想 吃 早饭 吗?

Come <u>get</u> your *cereal*.
lái <u>ná</u> nǐ-de *mài-piàn-er*
来拿 你的 麦 片 儿。

When are we *eating* <u>lunch</u>?
shén-me shí-hòu *chī* <u>wǔ-fàn</u>
什 么 时 候 吃 午 饭?

What <u>would you like to eat</u>?
nǐ <u>xiǎng chī</u> **shén-me**
你 想 吃 什 么?

You have *not* <u>eaten</u> **anything**.
nǐ shěn-me **dōu** *méi* <u>chī</u>
你 什 么 都 没 吃。

Dinner is ready (to eat).
<u>chī</u> *wǎn-fàn* le
吃 晚 饭 了。

Please **sit down** at the *dinner table*.
zuò dào *fàn-zhuō* qián
坐 到 饭 桌 前。
qián= in front

<u>Get close to</u> *the table*.
kào-<u>jìn</u> *zhuō-zi*
靠 近 桌 子。

Don't <u>put</u> your **elbows** *on the table*.
bié bǎ **gē-bó zhǒu** <u>fàng</u> *zài zhuō-zi* shàng
别 把 胳 膊 肘 放 在 桌 子 上。

Would you like (*to eat*) a <u>snack</u>?
nǐ xiǎng *chī* <u>líng-shí</u> ma
你 想 吃 零 食 吗?

Help your<u>self</u>.
<u>zì-jǐ</u> lái
自 己 来。
lái=come

Do you *want* to eat <u>bacon</u> or **potatoes**?
xiǎng chī <u>xūn-ròu</u> hái shì **tǔ-dòu**
想 吃 熏 肉 还 是 土 豆?

Make/Fix your<u>self</u> a **sandwich**.
zì-jǐ zuò <u>yí gè</u> **sān-míng-zhì**
自 己 做 一 个 三 明 治。

Do you **still** *want* more <u>to eat</u>?
hái *xiǎng* <u>chī</u> ma
还 想 吃 吗?

May I have *a little* **more** <u>carrots</u>?
wǒ néng zài **yào** *yì-diǎn-er* <u>hú-luó-bo</u> ma
我 能 再 要 一 点 儿 胡 萝 卜 吗?

I'll **take** <u>a little</u> more *cereal*.
wǒ zài **yào** <u>yì-diǎn-er</u> *mài-piàn*
我 再 要 一 点 儿 麦 片。

Is there *still* any <u>left</u> for me?
hái **yǒu** <u>shèng</u> de gěi wǒ ma
还 有 剩 的 给 我 吗?

I <u>don't want</u> any more.
wǒ <u>bú-yào</u> le
我 不 要 了。

May I have a **taste**?
wǒ <u>néng</u> **cháng-chang** ma
我 能 尝 尝 吗?

I cannot **eat** any more.
wǒ **chī** bú xià le
我 吃 不 下 了。
xià = have the capacity

I've had enough.
wǒ <u>bǎo-le</u>
我 饱 了。
bǎo-le =I'm full.

There is <u>no</u> more.
méi-yǒu le
没 有 了。

Would you <u>pass</u> the **salt**.
bǎ **yán** <u>dì-gěi</u> wǒ
把 盐 递 给 我.

Use your <u>fork</u>, *knife* and *spoon*.
yòng nǐ-de <u>chā-zi</u>, *dāo-zi* hé *sháo*
用 你 的 叉 子, 刀 子 和 勺。

Don't **squeeze** the *banana* in your *hand*.
bié yòng *shǒu* **jǐ** *xiāng-jiāo*
别 用 手 挤 香 蕉。

28

Be careful of the <u>pits</u>.
xiǎo-xīn yǒu <u>hú</u>
小 心 有 核。

Let me <u>cut</u> your **meat**.
wǒ bāng nǐ <u>qiē</u> **ròu**
我 帮 你 切 肉。

Don't <u>drink</u> so *fast*.
bié <u>hē</u> zhè-me *kuài*
别 喝 这 么 快。

Eat just <u>a little</u>. *Try it.*
chī <u>yì-diǎn-er</u>. *shì-shi*
吃 一 点 儿. 试试。

(The food) **really** <u>smells good</u>.
zhēn <u>xiāng</u>
真 香。
xiāng = fragrant, smells good

Is it good <u>to eat</u>?
néng <u>chī</u> ma
能 吃 吗?

The **coffee** has a <u>bitter</u> taste.
kā-fēi shì <u>kǔ-de</u>
咖啡 是 苦 的。

The pudding is **too**/ <u>sweet</u>/ *salty*/.
bù-dīng **tài**/ <u>tián</u>/ *xián*/
布 丁 太/ 甜/ 咸/。

The **sauce** is <u>bland</u>.
tiáo-liào hěn <u>dàn</u>
调 料 很 淡。

The **steak** is <u>juicy</u>.
niú-pái <u>duō zhī</u>
牛 排 多 汁。
zhī = juice

Do you **like** the <u>cheese</u>?
nǐ **xǐ-huān** <u>nǎi-lào</u> ma
你 喜 欢 奶 酪 吗?

Would you like <u>to drink</u> *tea*?
xiǎng <u>hē</u> *chá* ma
想 喝茶 吗?

What would you like to/ <u>drink</u>/ **eat**/?
nǐ **xiǎng** / <u>hē</u> / **chī** / diàn shén-me
你 想 / 喝/ 吃/ 点 什 么?

I'll have…
wǒ xiǎng yào …
我 想 要…

29

Mealtime_____chī fàn shí jiān 吃饭时间

Eat your spinach.
chī bō-cài
吃 菠 菜 。

I **like** string beans.
wǒ **xǐ-huān** dòu-jiǎo
我 喜 欢 豆 角。

Don't speak!
bié shuō-huà
别 说 话 ！

Don't speak with your *mouth* full.
zuǐ lǐ yǒu dōng-xi de shí-hòu **bié** shuō-huà
嘴 里 有 东 西 的 时 候 别 说 话 。

Pour the milk in the *glass*.
bǎ niú-nǎi **dào** zài *bēi-zi* lǐ
把 牛奶 倒在 杯子里。

You *can* **feed** yourself.
nǐ *néng* zì-jǐ **chī**
你 能 自 己 吃。

Cut the *bread* carefully.
xiǎo-xīn **qiē** *miàn-bāo*
小 心 切 面 包。

Don't spill the *water*.
bié bǎ *shuǐ* sǎ le
别 把 水 洒 了。

Why must you eat so *much*?
nǐ **wèi-shén-me** chī zhè-me *duō*
你 为 什 么 吃 这 么 多?

Finish (eating) your *dinner*.
bǎ *fàn* chī **wán**
把 饭 吃完。

Finish (*drinking*) your orange juice.
bǎ jú-zi-shǔi *hē* **wán**
把 桔 子 水 喝完。

Have you **finished** eating?
chī **wán** le ma
吃 完 了 吗?

Have you ever eaten **Chinese** *food*?
nǐ chī-guò **zhōng-guó** *fàn* ma
你 吃 过 中 国 饭 吗?

You have <u>eaten</u> *everything* on your **plate**.
nǐ bǎ **pán-zi** lǐ de *dōng-xi dōu* chī guāng le
你 把 盘子里的 东 西 都 吃 光 了。
guāng le = nothing is left

Here <u>comes</u> the pizza!　　That was **delicious**!　Delicious!
pī sā <u>lái</u> le　　　　　　hěn **hǎo-chī**　　　hǎo-chī
披萨 来 了!　　　　　　　很 好 吃!　　　　好 吃!

What <u>a</u> good **dinner**!　　　　　**Thank you** for <u>dinner</u>.
zhè **dùn** **fàn** zhēn hǎo　　　　**xiè-xie nǐ** qǐng wǒ <u>chī-fàn</u>
这 顿 饭 真 好!　　　　　　谢 谢 你 请 我 吃饭。

All gone! (<u>Nothing is left</u>)
dōu chī <u>guāng</u> le
都 吃 光 了!

Enjoy your meal!　Eat slowly!
hǎo hāo chī fàn　nǐ màn-mān chī
好 好 吃饭!　你 慢 慢 吃!
xiǎng-shòu = enjoy　màn-mān chī = eat slowly

31

Spare the rod and spoil the child. hái-zi bù dǎ bù chéng cái
孩 子 不 打 不 成 材.

Conversation

huì-huà 会 话

These are the pages you use to explain, persuade, and coax your child.
When all else fails, you can always say:

Because I said so! **yīn-wéi wǒ shuō guò** 因 为 我 说 过!

What is <u>that</u>?
<u>nà</u> shì **shén-me**
那 是 什 么?

 It's a **horse**.
nà shì yì-pí **mǎ**
那 是 一 匹 马。

What do you <u>hear</u>?
nǐ <u>tīng-jiàn</u> **shén-me** lā
你 听 见 什 么 啦?
lā – exclamation, question

What a <u>noise</u>!
zhēn <u>chǎo</u>
真 吵!

Did I **frighten** you?
wǒ **xià-zháo** nǐ le ma
我 吓 着 你 了 吗?

What are you saying?
nǐ shuō shén-me
你 说 什 么?

What did you say?
nǐ shuō le shén-me
你 说 了 什 么?

I'm **listening**.
wǒ zài **tīng**
我 在 听。

How **beautifully** you sing!
nǐ chàng de zhēn **hǎo-tīng**
你 唱 得 真 好 听!

How talkative you are!
nǐ zhè-me duō huà
你 这 么 多 话!

Come on! Sit up. (*straight*)
lái, zuò zhí
来, 坐 直。

Sit on my **lap**.
zuò zài wǒ **tuǐ shàng**
坐 在 我 腿 上。

Raise your head.
Tái-tóu
抬 头。

Look how strong!
kàn duó yǒu jìn
看 多 有 劲!

jìn = strength

Take it.
ná zhè
拿 着。

Hold the rattle.
ná zhè bō-làng-gǔ
拿 着 拨 浪 鼓。

Let go!
fàng-shǒu
放 手!

fàng-shǒu = let go

33

What are you <u>looking at</u>?
nǐ zài <u>kàn</u> **shén-me**
你在 看 什么?

What are you <u>thinking</u> about?
nǐ zài <u>xiǎng</u> **shén-me**
你在 想 什 么?

You're <u>dreaming</u>.
nǐ zài <u>zuò-mèng</u>
你 在 做 梦。

Move your <u>arms</u>.
dòng-dòng nǐ-de <u>gē-bo</u>
动 动 你的胳膊。

Who am I?
wǒ shì **shuí**
我 是 谁?

Who is/ he/ she/?
tā/ tā/ shì **shuí**
他//她/ 是 谁?

Who is it?
shì **shuí**
是 谁?

I **know** you.
wǒ **rèn-shi** nǐ
我 认识 你。

I don't **know** you.
wǒ bú **rèn-shi** nǐ
我 不认识 你。

It's your/ **older brother**/ <u>older sister</u>/.
zhè shì nǐ-de/ **gē-ge** / <u>jiě-jie</u>/.
这 是 你 的/ 哥哥/ 姐 姐/。

It's your/ **younger brother**/ <u>younger sister</u>/.
zhè shì nǐ-de/ **dì-di**/ <u>mèi-mei</u>/
这 是 你 的/弟 弟/妹 妹/。

(In Chinese, there are different words for older/younger siblings.)

/He/ She/ is **tall**.
/tā/ tā/ hěn **gāo**
/他/ 她/ 很 高。

It is/ **large**/ small/.
zhè/ hěn **dà**/ hěn xiǎo/
这/ 很 大/ 很 小/。

You have **eyes** *just like* your daddy's.
nǐ-de **yǎn-jīng** *zhēn xiàng* nǐ bà-ba
你 的 眼 睛 真 像 你 爸 爸。

Here is your *nose*, ear, mouth.
zhè shì nǐ-de *bí-zi*, ěr-duō, zuǐ-bā
这 是 你 的 鼻 子, 耳 朵, 嘴 巴。

What a **long** story!
hǎo **cháng** de gù-shì
好 长 的 故 事!

Smile!
xiào-yí-xiào
笑 一 笑!

I **want** to take your picture.
wǒ **xiǎng** gěi nǐ zhào xiàng
我 想 给 你 照 相。

Let me *rub* your tummy.
ràng wǒ gěi nǐ *róu-róu* dù-zi
让 我 给 你 揉 揉 肚 子。

You **like** that, don't you?
nǐ **xǐ-huān** nà-ge, shì-bú-shì
你 喜 欢 那 个, 是 不 是?

Where are you going?
nǐ qù **nǎ-er**
你 去 哪 儿?

Stand up.
zhàn qǐ-lái
站 起 来。

35

Conversation _____ huì-huà 会话

Look at...   Do you see...?
kàn...   nǐ kàn-jiàn ... le mā
看......   你看见......了吗?

Turn around. (child's self)   **What** do you *have* in your mouth?
zhuǎn shēn   nǐ zuǐ lǐ *yǒu* **shén-me**
转　身。   你 嘴 里 有 什 么?
                                   lǐ = in

              You cannot **put** that *in* your mouth.
                    bié **fàng** zuǐ *lǐ*
                    别 放 嘴 里 。

No kicking!   No splashing!
bié tī   bié jiàn shuǐ
别 踢!   别 溅 水!

No **biting**!   No **crying**!
bié **yǎo**   bié **kū**
别 咬!   别 哭!

Don't kick me!   Here's your **toy**.
bié tī wǒ   gěi nǐ **wán-jù**
别 踢 我!   给 你 玩 具。
                                   gěi = give

36

You're <u>getting</u> me <u>wet</u>!
nǐ bǎ wǒ <u>nòng shī</u> le
你 把 我 弄 湿 了！

Don't <u>cry</u>.
bié <u>kū</u>
别 哭。

Why are you <u>crying</u>?
nǐ **wèi-shén-me** <u>kū</u>
你 为 什 么 哭？

Where is the <u>rattle</u>?
<u>bō-làng-gǔ</u> zài **nǎ-er**
拨 浪 鼓 在 哪儿？

Where are the <u>blocks</u>?
<u>jī-mù</u> zài **nǎ-er**
积 木 在 哪儿？

Would you **like** to <u>play</u> with the *ball*?
nǐ **xiǎng** <u>wán</u> *qiú* ma
你 想 玩 球 吗？

Come to mommy.
dào mā-mā zhè **lái**
到 妈妈 这来。

We're <u>going</u> to visit (*to see*) **grandma**.
wǒ-men yào <u>qù</u> *kàn* **nǎi-nāi**
我 们 要 去 看 奶 奶。

We're going to **show** her <u>how big</u> you've *grown*.
ràng tā **kàn-kàn** nǐ *zhǎng* <u>duó dà</u> le
让 她 看 看 你 长 多 大 了。
ràng = let, allow

37

Look <u>how</u> you go! (*walk*)   <u>Let's</u> **see** how you *walk*.
kàn nǐ <u>zěn-me</u> *zǒu-lù*   <u>ràng</u> wǒ **kàn-kàn** nǐ zěn-me *zǒu-lù*
看 你 怎 么 走 路!   让 我 看 看 你 怎 么 走 路。

Look at those <u>teeth</u>!   Do your <u>teeth hurt</u>?
kàn zhè-xiē <u>yá</u>   nǐ <u>yá-téng</u> ma
看 这 些 牙!   你 牙 疼 吗?

Bang the <u>drum</u>!   **Ring** the <u>bell</u>!   **Clap**! <u>Play</u> another *song*.
qiāo <u>gǔ</u>   **yáo** <u>líng</u>   **pài-shǒu**, zài <u>tán</u> *yì-shǒu gē*
敲 鼓!   摇 铃!   拍 手! 再 弹 一 首 歌。
             yáo = rattle   yì-shǒu gē = a song

Not so <u>loud</u>!   What <u>beautiful music</u>!
bié zhè-me <u>dà-shēng</u>   zhēn <u>hǎo-tīng</u>
别 这 么 大 声!   真 好 听!
          hǎo-tīng = good listen
          zhēn = really

Here is a *baby* <u>like</u> you.   **Who** is that in the <u>mirror</u>?
zhè ge *wá-wa* <u>xiàng</u> nǐ   **shuí** zài <u>jìng-zi</u> lǐ
这 个 娃 娃 像 你。   谁 在 镜 子里?
                                  lǐ = in

Where are/ the **feet**/ the *eyes*/ of the <u>baby</u>?
<u>wá-wa</u> dè/ **jiǎo** / *yǎn-jīng*/ zài nǎ
娃娃 的/ 脚/ 眼 睛/ 在 哪？

Let's **go for a stroll** in your <u>carriage</u>.
zuò <u>xiǎo-chē</u> **sàn-sàn-bù**
坐 小 车 散 散 步。

We have to **go** to the <u>doctor's</u>.
wǒ-men yào **qù** kàn yī-shēng
我 们 要 去 看 医 生。

Don't *be afraid*. <u>It's</u> O.K.
bié *hài-pà*. <u>méi</u> guān-xi
别 害 怕。没 关 系。
guān-xi = matter, problem
méi = no, not have

I'm **coming**! I'm coming to <u>get</u> you!
wǒ **lái** la. wǒ lái <u>zhuā</u> nǐ
我 来 了！我 来 抓 你！
zhuā = grab, get

Now I've <u>gotcha</u>!
wǒ <u>dǎi zhù</u> nǐ là
我 逮 住 你 啦！
dǎi zhù = catch

Don't you <u>like</u> … (sth)?
nǐ bù <u>xǐ-huān</u> … ma
你不喜欢 …… 吗？

Don't you <u>want</u>…(sth)?
nǐ bù <u>xiǎng yào</u> … ma
你 不 想 要 …. 吗？

Don't you <u>want</u>…(*to do* sth)?
nǐ bù <u>xiǎng</u> *zuò* … ma
你 不 想 做……吗？

39

Take my **hand**.
zhuā-zhè wǒ-de **shǒu**
抓 着 我 的 手。
zhuā-zhè = take hold of (hand)

Let's <u>take a little walk</u>.
wǒ-men <u>sàn-sàn-bù</u>
我 们 散 散 步。

Sit on your <u>chair</u>.
zuò zài nǐ-de <u>yǐ-zī</u> shàng
坐 在 你 的 椅 子 上。

Be careful./ **Watch** the <u>step</u>.
xiǎo-xīn <u>jiǎo-xià</u>
小 心 脚 下。

Climb the <u>stairs</u>.
pá <u>lóu-tī</u>
爬 楼 梯。

Come down the <u>stairs</u> *carefully*.
xiǎo-xīn **xià** <u>lóu-tī</u>
小 心 下 楼 梯。

Turn <u>around</u>.
zhuǎn <u>shēn</u>
转 身。

Don't turn around (half-way).
bié huí-tóu
别 回 头。
huí-tóu = turn head

Put your *foot* in the <u>pants</u>.
bǎ *jiǎo* **fàng** dào <u>kù-zi</u> lǐ
把 脚 放 到 裤 子 里。

Pull your **hand** *out* of the <u>sleeve</u>.
bǎ **shǒu** cóng <u>xiù-zi</u> lǐ shēn *chū-lái*
把 手 从 袖 子 里 伸 出 来。
shēn = pull out, stick out

Daddy <u>will</u> *put on* your pajamas.
bà-ba <u>huì</u> gěi nǐ *chuān* shuì-yī
爸 爸 会 给 你 穿 睡 衣。
shuì-yī = pajamas

40

Go and <u>get</u> your *new shoes*.
qù bǎ nǐ-de *xīn-xié* <u>ná lai</u>
去 把 你 的 新 鞋 拿 来。
ná = take, fetch

Go and <u>get</u>/ the blocks/ *the ball*.
qù bǎ/ jī-mù/ *qiú*/ <u>ná lái</u>
去 把/ 积 木/ 球/ 拿 来。

What do you *have* in your <u>hand</u>?
nǐ-de <u>shǒu-lǐ</u> *yǒu* **shén-me**
你 的 手 里 有 什 么?

Give it to me.
gěi wǒ
给 我。

Let go of it.
sōng shǒu
松 手。

Don't <u>touch</u> it.
bié <u>pèng</u>
别 碰。

Don't <u>break</u> it.
bié <u>nòng huài</u> le
别 弄 坏 了。

Stay <u>seated</u>.
zuò zhe
坐 着。

<u>Take</u> **good** <u>care</u> of your *teddy bear*.
hǎo-hāo <u>ài-hù</u> nǐ-de *xiǎo-xióng*
好 好 爱 护 你 的 小 熊。

Feed your <u>doll</u>.
wèi nǐ-de <u>wá-wa</u> **chī-fàn**
喂 你 的 娃 娃 吃 饭。

Give/ him/ her/ <u>a cup of tea</u>.
gěi/ tā/ tā/ <u>yī-bēi chá</u>
给 他/她 一 杯 茶。

Pet the *dog* <u>gently</u>.
Qīng-qīng **pāi** *gǒu*
轻 轻 拍 狗。

Stop/ *kicking*/ <u>hitting</u>/!
bié/ *tī*/ <u>dǎ</u>/
别/ 踢/ 打 /！

Stop/ *biting*/ <u>crying</u>/!
bié/ *yǎo*/ <u>kū</u>/
别/ 咬/ 哭 /！

Stop!/ Stop it! (at this minute)
zhù shǒu
住 手！

Stop misbehaving. (generally)
bié nào le
别 闹 了。

That **hurts** (me).
hěn **téng**
很 疼。

Don't *go in*.
bié *jìn-qù*
别 进 去。

Give me your <u>hand</u>.
bǎ <u>shǒu</u> **gěi** wǒ
把 手 给 我。

Don't make <u>too much</u> *noise*.
bié <u>tài</u> *chǎo*
别 太 吵。

Quiet, <u>please</u>.
<u>qǐng</u> **ān-jìng**
请 安 静。

Be quiet.
ān-jìng
安 静。

Stay there. (**Don't** <u>leave</u>.)
bié <u>zǒu</u>
别 走。

42

I'm **busy** <u>now</u>.
wǒ <u>xiàn-zài</u> hěn **máng**
我 现 在 很 忙。

I'm in a <u>hurry</u>.
wǒ hěn <u>jí</u>
我 很 急。

I **must** <u>go</u>.
wǒ **bì-xū** <u>zǒu</u> le
我 必 须 走 了。

I'll **come back** <u>soon</u>.
wǒ hěn-<u>kuài</u> jiù **huí-lái**
我 很 快 就 回 来。
huí-lái = return

Wait! (a minute)
Děng-yì-děng
等 一 等!

Just a moment, **please**.
qǐng děng-yí-xià
请 等 一 下。

Don't <u>move</u>.
bié <u>dòng</u>
别 动。

Don't <u>go away</u>.
bié <u>zǒu-kāi</u>
别 走 开。

Come away from <u>there</u>.
lí-kài <u>nà-lǐ</u>
离 开 那 里。

Stop doing <u>that</u>.
bié nòng <u>nà-ge</u>
别 弄 那 个。

Do what I tell you!
tīng huà
听 话!
tīng huà = listen instruction

(OR)

Do as you are told! <u>Listen!</u>
tīng huà
听 话!

Don't *give* me trouble.
bié *gěi* wǒ tiān má-fan
别 给 我 添 麻 烦。

Don't fight!   Take turns.
bié dǎ-jià   lún-liú lái
别 打 架!   轮 流 来。

Don't bother/ him/ her/ it/.
  bié fán/ tā/ tā/ tā/
  别 烦 /他/ 她/ 它/。
  fán – used with adults

Don't *bother* him!   **Don't** *tease* the cat!
bié *dòu* tā   **bié** *dòu* māo
别 逗 他!   别 逗 猫!
  dòu = tease, bother (used with children or pets)

Don't *touch* that. It's dirty.   **Don't** pick that up.
bié *pèng*. nà hěn zāng   **bié** jiǎn nà-ge
别 碰。 那 很 脏。   别 捡 那 个。

Open the door.   **Close** the door.   **Don't** *lock* the door.
  kāi mén   **guān** mén   **bié** *suǒ* mén
  开 门。   关 门。   别 锁 门。

44

Don't *open* the <u>window.</u>
bié *kāi* <u>chuāng-hù</u>
别 开 窗 户。

Don't <u>lean out</u> the *window.*
bié bǎ shēn-zi <u>tàn dào</u> *chuāng-hù* <u>wài</u>
别 把 身 子 探 到 窗 户 外。

Put the *box* over <u>there.</u>
bǎ *hé-zi* **fàng** zài <u>nà-li</u>
把 盒 子 放 在 那 里。

Put the *shoes* <u>back</u> in their place.
bǎ *xié* **fàng** <u>huí</u> yuán-chù
把 鞋 放 回 原 处。

yuán-chù = original place

Jump!/ **Don't** jump!
tiào/ **bié** tiào
跳!/ 别 跳!

Don't *run.* Go <u>slower.</u>
bié *pào.* <u>màn</u> diǎn-er
别 跑。 慢 点 儿。

Hurry!/ **Don't** <u>hurry!</u>
kuài/ **bié** <u>jí</u>
快! / 别 急!
kuài = fast, quick; jí = hurry

Slowly!
màn-màn-de
慢 慢 的!

You **will** <u>trip.</u>
nǐ **huì** <u>bàn-dǎo</u>
你 会 拌 倒.

We **must** hurry.
wǒ-mén **bì-xū** kuài-diǎn-er
我 们 必 须 快 点 儿。

We **must** go.
wǒ-mén **bì-xū** <u>zǒu</u> le
我 们 必 须 走 了。

Don't *write* on the <u>wall</u>.
bié wǎng <u>qiáng</u> shàng *xiě-zi*
别 往 墙 上 写 字。
wǎng = in the direction

Step <u>back</u>.
wǎng <u>hòu-tuì</u>
往 后 退。
wǎng = in the direction of

Don't *touch* the <u>stove</u>.
bié *pèng* <u>lú-zi</u>
别 碰 炉 子。

Don't *play* with <u>matches</u>!
bié *wán* <u>huǒ-chái</u>
别 玩 火 柴!

You **will** *burn* <u>yourself</u>.
nǐ **huì** *tàng-zháo* <u>zì-ji</u>
你 会 烫 着 自 己。

Did you *burn* yourself?
nǐ *tàng-zháo* le ma
你 烫 着 了 吗?

Stay away from <u>the stairs</u>!
 lí-kāi <u>lóu-tī</u>
离 开 楼 梯!
lí-kāi = go away from

Don't *cross* the <u>street</u>.
bié *guò* <u>mǎ-lù</u>
别 过 马 路。

Stay away from/ the *barbecue*/ the <u>street</u>/.
bié kào-jìn/ *kǎo-ròu-jī* / <u>mǎ-lù</u>/
别 靠 近 烤 肉 机/马 路。

Hold onto the <u>carriage</u>.
zhuā-zhù <u>xiǎo-chē</u>
抓 住 小 车。

Wait for the <u>green</u> traffic <u>light</u>.
děng <u>lǜ-dēng</u>
等 绿 灯。

46

Look *left and right* <u>before</u> crossing the street.
<u>xiān</u> **kàn-kàn** *zuǒ-yòu* zài guò mǎ-lù
先　看　看　左　右　再　过　马　路。

From *now* on, be <u>careful</u>!
cóng *xiàn-zài* qǐ yào <u>xiǎo-xīn</u>
从　现　在　起　要　小　心!

Hold it by the <u>handle</u>.
zhuā-zhù <u>fú-shǒu</u>
抓　住　扶　手。

Hold it with <u>two hands</u>.
yòng <u>liǎng-zhī-shǒu</u> **zhuā-zhù**
用　两　只　手　抓　住。

Pay attention to what you are doing.
zhuān-xīn zuò-shì
专　心　做　事。
zhuān-xīn = concentrate (your) mind

Don't *drop* it on the <u>ground</u>.
bié *diào* zài <u>dì-shàng</u>
别　掉　在　地　上。
dì = ground, floor; shàng = above, on the

Don't *grab* <u>that</u>.
bié *zhuā* <u>nà-ge</u>
别　抓　那　个。

Don't *cut* your <u>finger</u>.
bié *qiē* <u>shǒu</u>
别　切　手。

The **knife** is <u>sharp</u>.
dāo-zi hěn <u>kuài</u>
刀　子　很　快。
kuài = quick, fast, sharp

47

Because I <u>said</u> so!
yīn-wéi wǒ <u>shuō-guò</u>
因 为 我 说 过!
shuō = say

Because that's <u>the way it is</u>!
yīn-wéi <u>jiù shì zhè yàng</u>
因 为 就 是 这 样!

What do you/ <u>think</u>/ **say**/?
nǐ/ <u>rèn-wéi</u>/ **shuō**/ nā
你/ 认 为/ 说 / 呢?

Do you <u>think</u>....?
nǐ <u>rèn-wéi</u>...
你 认 为......?

Please *bring* me the <u>mop</u>.
qǐng bǎ <u>tuō-bǎ</u> *nǎ-lai*
请 把 拖 把 拿 来。

Can you *help* me with <u>lunch</u>?
nǐ **néng** *bāng* wǒ zuò <u>wǔ-fàn</u> ma
你 能 帮 我 做 午 饭 吗?

Can you <u>rock the baby</u>?
nǐ **néng** <u>yáo-yáo yīng-ér</u> ma
你 能 摇 摇 婴 儿 吗?
yīng-ér = infant, baby

May I **ask** you…(*why* you didn't eat your <u>breakfast</u>)?
wǒ xiǎng **wèn** nǐ… (nǐ *wèi-shén-me* méi chī <u>zǎo-fàn</u>)
我 想 问 你… (你 为 什 么 没 吃 早 饭)?

Tell your *younger brother* to <u>come upstairs</u>.
jiào *dì-di* <u>shàng lóu lái</u>
叫 弟 弟 上 楼 来。
dì-di = younger brother

Tell him he *should* <u>come</u>.
gào-sù tā tā *yīng-gāi* <u>lái</u>
告 诉 他 他 应 该 来。

Your **older sister** *should* <u>come in</u>.
nǐ **jiě-jiē** *yīng-gāi* <u>jìn-lái</u>
你 姐 姐 应 该 进 来。

jie-jie = older sister

I **want** to <u>see</u>/ him/ her/.
wǒ **xiǎng** <u>jiàn</u>/ tā/ tā/
我 想 见/ 他/ 她/。

You <u>have gotten</u> your **shirt** *dirty*.
nǐ <u>bǎ</u> **chèn-yī** <u>nòng</u> *zāng* le
你 把 衬 衣 弄 脏 了。

bǎ ... nòng = have gotten

Go to your **room** and <u>change to</u> a *shirt*.
dào nǐ-de **fáng-jiān** <u>huàn yí-jiàn</u> *chèn-yī*
到 你 的 房 间 换 一 件 衬 衣。

huàn yí-jiàn =change to a piece (of cloth)

Where is your **room**?
nǐ-de **fáng-jiān** zài *nǎ-er*
你 的 房 间 在 哪 儿?

What are you <u>doing</u>?
nǐ zài <u>zuò</u> **shén-me**
你 在 做 什 么?

Let him <u>do</u> it.
ràng tā <u>zuò</u>
让 他 做。

Lie <u>down</u>.
tǎng <u>xià</u>
躺 下。

Sit <u>down</u>. Remain seated. (Don't *get up*.)
zuò <u>xià</u>. bié *qǐ-lái*
坐 下。别 起 来。

49

Stand *up.* Keep **standing.**
zhàn *qǐ-lái.* **zhàn zhe**
站 起 来。站 着。
zhe – verbal suffix (-ing)

Did you do it **on purpose?**
nǐ shì **gù-yì** de ma
你 是 故 意 的 吗？

I want you to **tell** me the <u>truth.</u>
gēn wǒ **shuō** <u>shí-huà</u>
跟 我 说 实 话。

Please **speak** <u>a little more</u>/ *clearly*/ slowly/.
qǐng nǐ **shuō**/ *qīng-chu* diǎn-er/ màn <u>diǎn-er</u>/
请 你 说/ 清 楚 点 儿/ 慢 点 儿。

Listen <u>carefully.</u>
<u>zǐ-xì</u> **tīng** zhe
仔 细 听 着。

You are in a/ <u>bad</u>/ good/ **mood.**
nǐ **xīn-qíng**/ <u>bù-hǎo</u>/ hǎo/
你 心 情 / 不 好/ 好/。

Do you **promise** to be good?
nǐ **dá-yīng** tīng-huà ma
你 答 应 听 话 吗？
tīng-huà = listen to words, behave

Behave!/ Don't **misbehave!**
bié **hú-nào**
别 胡 闹！

Do you **understand** (<u>my words</u>)?
nǐ **míng-bái** <u>wǒ-de huà</u> ma
你 明 白 我 的 话 吗？

Don't be **naughty.**
bié **táo-qì**
别 淘 气。

You're *really* <u>stubborn</u>!
nǐ *zhēn* <u>gù-zhí</u>
你 真 固 执!

Don't/ <u>provoke</u> me/ try my patience/!
bié <u>rě</u> wǒ
别 惹 我!

Don't be <u>nervous</u>. (Calm down.)
bié <u>jǐn-zhāng</u>
别 紧 张。

Everything *will* be <u>all right</u>.
yí-qiè dōu *huì* <u>hǎo</u> de
一 切 都 会 好 的。

Don't *give up*! **Don't** <u>give in</u>!
bié *fàng-qì*. **bié** <u>ràng-bù</u>
别 放 弃! 别 让 步!

You have **bumped** your <u>nose</u>.
nǐ **pèng dào** <u>bí</u>-zi le
你 碰 到 鼻 子 了。

<u>Show</u> me **where** it *hurts*.
<u>zhǐ gěi</u> wǒ <u>kàn</u> **nǎ-lǐ** *téng*
指 给 我 看 哪 里 疼。
zhǐ gěi = point toward, direct

Rub it *with* your <u>hand</u>.
yòng <u>shǒu</u> **róu-róu**
用 手 揉 揉。

Open your <u>mouth</u>.
zhāng <u>zuǐ</u>
张 嘴。

Don't *put* the <u>pebble</u> *in* your **mouth**.
bié bǎ <u>xiǎo-shí-tóu</u> *fàng jìn* **zuǐ**-lǐ
别 把 小 石 头 放 进 嘴 里。
lǐ = inside; fàng jin = put in

51

Don't *make* faces.
bié *zuò* guǐ-liǎn
别 做 鬼 脸。

That will do you good.
nà jiāng duì nǐ yǒu hǎo-chù
那 将 对你有 好 处。
jiāng duì = will toward

Wipe your nose.
cā bí-zi
擦 鼻 子。

Breathe through (*using*) your nose.
yòng bí-zi **hū-xī**
用 鼻 子呼吸。

Don't *tell* me that …
bié *gào-sù* wǒ
别 告诉我……

Forget your *toy* for a moment.
zàn-shí **wàng-jì** nǐ-de *wán-jù*
暂 时 忘 记你的 玩具。

Play with your own *toys*.
wán nǐ-zi-jǐ de *wán-jù*
玩你自己 的 玩 具。

Don't **forget** (*to bring*) your crayons.
bié **wàng-le** *dài* nǐ-de là-bǐ
别 忘 了带你的 蜡 笔。

Come *with* me.
gēn wǒ **lái**
跟 我 来。

Immediately!
lì-kè
立 刻!

Go to the bathroom. (toilet)
shàng cè-suǒ
上 厕 所。

Go to the *bathroom* to wash.
qù *yù-shì* xǐ-yì-xǐ
去 浴 室 洗 一洗。

You *go* first.
nǐ xiān zǒu
你 先 走。

This way! *Follow* me!
zhè-biān. *gēn-zhe* wǒ
这 边! 跟 着 我!

/Can/*Can't*/ you do it yourself?
nǐ /**néng** / *bù-néng*/ zì-jǐ zuò ma
你/ 能 / 不 能/ 自 己 做 吗?

Go upstairs 'n *help* Grandma.
shàng-lóu qù *bāng* nǎi-nǎi
上 楼 去 帮 奶 奶。
shàng-lóu = (verb)

Play/ *downstairs*/ upstairs/.
zài *lóu-xià*/ lóu-shàng/ **wán**
在 楼 下/ 楼 上 玩。
lóu-shàng = (noun)

Play on the sidewalk.
zài rén-xíng-dào shàng **wán**
在 人 行 道 上 玩。

Go *outdoors*.
dào *wài-biān* **qù.**
到 外 边 去。

Come inside.
jìn-lái
进 来。
jìn = enter

Turn on the *DVD* player.
kāi *guāng-pán* jī
开 光 盘 机。

Don't turn off the light.
bié guān-dēng
别 关 灯。

Turn on the light.
kāi-dēng
开 灯。

It's *too* dark. (**in here**)
(**zhè-lǐ**) *tài* hēi le
这 里 太 黑 了。

That's (not) yours.
nà (bú) shì nǐ-de
那 (不) 是 你 的。

This is (not) yours.
zhè (bú) shì nǐ-de
这 (不) 是 你 的。

There is yours.
nǐ-de zài **nà-er**
你 的 在 那 儿。

You are **not allowed** to *eat* in the <u>living room</u>.
nǐ **bù-néng** zài <u>kè-tīng</u> lǐ *chī* dōng-xi
你 不 能 在 客 厅 里 吃 东 西。

Eat in the *kitchen* so that you don't <u>spot</u> the *rug*.
zài *chú-fáng* lǐ **chī**, miǎn-de <u>nòng-zāng</u> *dì-tǎn*
在 厨 房 里 吃，免 得 弄 脏 地 毯。

Don't be *afraid* to ask <u>questions</u>.
bié *pà* wèn <u>wèn-tí</u>.
别 怕 问 问 题。
wèn = ask

Don't *ask* me (again)!
bié (zài) *wèn* wǒ
别 (再) 问 我!

Don't *give* me...
bié *gěi* wǒ...
别 给 我......

<u>Wait</u> 'til I **come back**. Then we'll *talk*.
<u>děng</u> wǒ **huí-lái**, wǒ-mén zài *tán*
等 我 回 来, 我 们 再 谈。

Don't <u>disobey</u> me!
bié <u>bù-tīng-huà</u>
别 不 听 话!
bù-tīng-huà = not listen to my words

Do what you/ **like**/ **please**/. You're/ *responsible*/ <u>dependable</u>/.
suí biàn. nǐ shì/ *fù-zé de*/ <u>kě-kào de</u>/
随 便。你 是/ 负 责 的 /可 靠 的 /。
suí or suí biàn = please

54

Go *to* your <u>room</u>.
dào nǐ-de <u>fáng-jiān</u> **qù**
到 你 的 房 间 去。

Don't *quarrel* with one another.
bié *chǎo-jià*
别 吵 架。

Close the *refrigerator* <u>door</u>.
guān-shàng *bīng-xiāng* <u>mén</u>
关 上 冰 箱 门。

Take your time. (<u>Don't hurry</u>.)
màn-mān <u>lái</u>   (<u>bié jí</u>)
慢 慢 来。(别 急.)

Don't *forget* to **wipe** your <u>feet</u>.
bié *wàng-le* bǎ <u>jiǎo</u> **cā** gān-jìng
别 忘 了 把 脚 擦 干 净。

Don't **walk** *barefoot* <u>outside</u>.
bié *guāng-jiǎo* dào <u>wài-biān</u> **zǒu**
别 光 脚 到 外 边 走。

What *can* we <u>do</u>?
wǒ-mén *néng* <u>zuò</u> **shén-me**
我 们 能 做 什 么？

Let's **try** <u>together</u>.
wǒ-mén *yì-qǐ* **shì-shi**
我 们 一 起 试 试。

Tell me *what* <u>happened</u>.
gào-sù wǒ *fā-shēng* le *shén-me-shì*
告 诉 我 发 生 了 什 么 事。
shì = things

Don't *use* <u>dirty</u> words!
bié *yòng* <u>zāng-zì</u>
别 用 脏 字！
Watch your language!

55

You **always** *have* an <u>answer (reason)</u> for everything!
nǐ **zǒng** *yǒu* <u>lǐ-yóu</u>
你 总 有 理 由！

Lower the <u>radio</u>!
bǎ <u>shōu-yīn-jī</u> **guān xiǎo**
把 收 音 机 关 小！

Turn off the *television*.
guān *diàn-shì*
关 电 视。

You **may not** *watch* this <u>program</u>.
Nǐ **bù-néng** *kàn* zhè-gè <u>jié-mù</u>
你 不 能 看 这 个 节 目。

Do your <u>homework</u>.
zuò <u>gōng-kè</u>
做 功 课。

Are you about to **watch** *TV*?
Nǐ yào **kàn** *diàn-shì* ma
你 要 看 电 视 吗？

You cannot watch *TV* when you are <u>doing homework</u>!
nǐ <u>zuò gōng-kè</u> de shí-hòu **bù-néng kàn** *diàn-shì*
你 做 功 课 的 时 候 不 能 看 电 视！

Stop **talking** on the *phone*!
bié **jiǎng** *diàn-huà* la
别 讲 电 话 啦！
la – exclamation

Stop **using** the *computer*!
bié **yòng** *diàn-nǎo* la
别 用 电 脑 啦！

It's too *late* to <u>invite</u> **friends**.
tài *wǎn* le, bù-néng <u>qǐng</u> **péng-yǒu** lái le
太 晚 了，不 能 请 朋 友 来 了。

No <u>smoking</u>!
bié <u>chōu-yān</u>
别 抽 烟！

56

Your **book** is <u>overdue</u>.
nǐ jiè de **shū** <u>guò-qī</u> le
你 借 的 书 过 期 了。
jiè = borrow, lend

You have/ (sports) **practice**/ *music lessons*/ <u>today</u>.
nǐ <u>jīn-tiān</u> yǒu/ (tǐ-yù) **liàn-xí**/ *yīn-yuè kè*/
你 今 天 有 /(体 育) 练 习/ 音 乐 课/。

Who's been running up the *phone* <u>bill</u>?
shuí dǎ zhè-me duō *diàn-huà*? <u>zhàng-dān</u> zhè-me guì
谁 打 这 麽 多 电 话? 帐 单 这 麽 贵。
guì = expensive

You **should** *feed* the/ dog/ cat/ <u>now</u>.
nǐ <u>xiàn-zài</u> **yīng-gāi** *wèi*/ gǒu/ māo/
你 现 在 应 该 喂/ 狗/ 猫/。

It's **your turn** to take the *dog* for a <u>walk</u>.
lún dào nǐ <u>liù</u> *gǒu* le
轮 到 你 遛 狗 了。
liù = stroll

It's **your turn** to/ *carry out*/ *put out*/ the <u>garbage</u>.
lún dào nǐ bǎ <u>lā-jī</u> *ná-chū-qù*
轮 到 你 把 垃 圾 拿 出 去。

Can you *carry* the <u>dish</u>?
nǐ **néng** *ná* <u>pán-zi</u> ma
你 能 拿 盘 子 吗?

The **refrigerator** is off limits!
bié yòng **bīng-xiāng**
别 用 冰 箱 !

yòng = use

Take off the <u>head set</u>!
bǎ <u>ěr-jī</u> **zhāi-xià-lái**
把 耳 机 摘 下 来!

Come home <u>on time</u>!
<u>àn-shí</u> **huí-jiā**
按 时 回 家!

Don't <u>be late</u>!
bié <u>wǎn le</u>
别 晚 了!

I don't **want** to *hear* any <u>complaints</u>.
wǒ bù **xiǎng** *tīng* rèn-hé <u>bào-yuàn</u>
我 不 想 听 任 何 抱 怨。

It's/ all right/ O.K/. It *can* be <u>done</u>.
méi-guān-xi. *néng* <u>zuò-dào</u>
没 关 系, 能 做 到。

Not at all!
bù xíng
不 行 !

It's out of the question!
nà shì bù-kě-néng de
那 是 不 可 能 的!

I'd rather not. Let's not.
wǒ bù xiǎng zuò. wǒ-mén bié zuò le
我 不 想 做。 我 们 别 做 了

zuò = do

Put on your <u>seat belt</u>.
xì shàng <u>ān-quán-dài</u>
系 上 安 全 带。

Because I <u>said</u> so!
yīn-wéi wǒ <u>shuō guò</u>
因 为 我 说 过!

Many hands make light work.   rén duō hǎo bàn-shì
人 多 好 办 事

Helping at Home   bāng-máng zuò jiā-wù   帮忙做家务

Children are happiest when imitating adults in their lives. This includes the work they do. You and your children working together are a natural setting for speaking Chinese together.

I need your help.   wǒ xū-yào nǐ bāng-máng
我 需 要 你 帮 忙。

Help me <u>set the table</u>.
bāng wǒ <u>bǎi zhuō-zi</u>
帮 我 摆 桌 子。

Set the table, **please**.
qǐng <u>bǎ zhuō-zi bǎi hǎo</u>
请 把 桌 子 摆 好。

<u>Spread</u> the **tablecloth**, and put on *napkins*, please.
qǐng nǐ <u>pū</u> **zhuō-bù,** bǎi *cān-jīn*
请 你 铺 桌 布, 摆 餐 巾。

59

Helping at Home _____ bāng-máng zuò jiā-wù 帮忙做家务

Clear the <u>table</u>, *please*.
qǐng **shōu-shi** <u>zhuō-zi</u>
请　收　拾　桌　子。
shōu-shi = pack, put in order

Help me/ *wash*/ *dry*/ the **dishes**.
bāng wǒ/ *xǐ*/ <u>cā gān</u>/ **pán-zi**
帮　我/洗/　擦　干/盘　子。
cā gān = wipe, dry

The **sink** is *filled* with <u>dishes</u>.
shuǐ-chí lǐ duì *mǎn* le <u>pán-zi</u>
水　池　里　堆　满　了　盘　子。
mǎn = full, expire

Help me *wash* the <u>clothes</u>.
bāng wǒ *xǐ* <u>yī-fu</u>
帮　我　洗衣　服。

Help me <u>make the bed</u>.
bāng wǒ zhěng-lǐ <u>chuáng-pù</u>
帮　我　整　理　床　铺。

Did you <u>make your bed</u>?
nǐ-de <u>chuáng</u> zhěng-lǐ hǎo-le ma
你的　床　整　理　好了吗？

Why <u>not</u>?
Wèi-shén-me <u>bù</u>
为　什么　不？

Good/ girl!/ boy!/ (child)
hǎo <u>hái-zi</u>
好孩子！

You make a lot of <u>work</u> for me!
nǐ jìng gěi wǒ zhǎo <u>shì-er</u>
你净给我找事儿！
jìng = always; zhǎo = find, look for

Mom's <u>sweeping</u> the <u>floor</u>.
mā-ma zài <u>sǎo-dì</u>
妈妈　在　扫　地。

Daddy is *vacuuming* the <u>rug</u>.
bà-ba zài gěi <u>dì-tǎn</u> *xī-chén*
爸爸在给地毯吸尘。

The *vacuum cleaner* is <u>loud</u>.
xī-chén-qì hěn <u>chǎo</u>
吸尘器　很　吵。

60

Helping at Home ___bāng-máng zuò jiā-wù 帮忙做家务

What <u>dust</u>!
hǎo-duō <u>huī-chén</u>
好 多 灰 尘！

Let's do some <u>dusting</u>!
wǒ-mén dǎn-dǎn huī
我 们 掸 掸 灰！

Hold the dust cloth in your <u>hand</u>, and *rub*.
yòng <u>shǒu</u> **ná-zhé** mǒ-bù *cā*
用 手 拿 着 抹 布 擦。
mǒ-bù = dust cloth

That's <u>right</u>.
<u>duì</u> le
对 了。

I'm **sewing** a <u>blouse</u> for you.
wǒ gěi nǐ **féng** <u>chèn-shān</u>
我 给 你 缝 衬 衫。
gěi = for, give

Help Daddy *make* <u>lunch</u>.
bāng bà-ba *zuò* <u>wǔ-fàn</u>
帮 爸 爸 做 午 饭。

Mommy's *baking* a <u>cake</u>.
mā-ma zài *kǎo* <u>dàn-gāo</u>
妈 妈 在 烤 蛋 糕。

Do you **want to help** me *bake* <u>cookies</u>?
nǐ **xiǎng bāng** wǒ *kǎo* <u>bǐng-gān</u> ma
你 想 帮 我 烤 饼 干 吗？

Pour in the <u>flour</u>.
bǎ <u>miàn-fěn</u> **dào jìn-lái**
把 面 粉 倒 进 来。
jìn-lái = enter container

I'm **beating** the <u>eggs</u>.
wǒ zài **tiáo** <u>jī-dàn</u>
我 在 调 鸡 蛋。

61

I'm **mixing** the *sugar* and butter.
wǒ zài **tiáo** *táng* hé huáng-yóu
我 在 调 糖 和 黄 油。

Roll the dough.
gǔn miàn-tuán
滚 面 团。

Do we **need** baking powder?
wǒ-mén **xū-yào** fā-xiào-fěn ma
我 们 需 要 发 酵 粉 吗？

We **bake**/ it/ them/ in the oven.
wǒ-mén zài kǎo-xiāng lǐ **kǎo**/ tā/ tā-mén/
我 们 在 烤 箱 里 烤/它/它 们/。

Set the clock for *half an hour*.
bǎ jì-shí-qì **shè dào** *bàn-xiǎo-shí*
把 记时器 设 到 半 小 时。

The **cookies** are done.
bǐng-gān hǎo-le
饼 干 好 了。

You **can help** me/ *sort*/ fold/ the laundry.
nǐ **néng bāng** wǒ/ *zhěng-lǐ*/ dié / yī-fu
你 能 帮 我 /整 理/ 迭 /衣 服。
yī-fu = cloth

After cleaning, we can *read* a story.
dá-sǎo qīng-jié **hòu**, wǒ-mén *dú* yí-gè gù-shi
打 扫 清 洁 后，我 们 读 一 个 故 事。
gù-shi = story

62

Before playing, you *must* straighten your room.
wán-er **yǐ-qián,** nǐ *bì-xū* bǎ nǐ-de fáng-jiān zhěng-lǐ hǎo
玩儿 以 前，你必须 把你 的 房 间 整 理 好。

wán-er = play, have fun; fáng-jiān = room

Put all your *pots* **back** in the cabinet.
bǎ suǒ-yǒu de *guō* **fàng-huí** guì-chú li
把 所 有 的 锅 放 回 柜 橱 里。

Would you **like** to go shopping with me?
nǐ **xiǎng** hé wǒ qù mǎi dōng-xi ma
你 想 和 我 去 买 东 西 吗？

dōng =east; xi = west; dōng-xi = anything (from east to west)

We **need** to *buy* something to eat.
wǒ-mén **xū-yào** *mǎi* chī-de
我 们 需 要 买 吃 的。

You **need** *new* clothes.
nǐ **xū-yào** *xīn* yī-fu
你 需 要 新 衣 服。

Here is your allowance. (a little money)
zhè shì nǐ-de líng-yòng-qián
这 是 你 的 零 用 钱。

Can you help me wrap the **present**?
nǐ néng bāng wǒ bāo **lǐ-wù** ma
你 能 帮 我 包 礼 物 吗？

63

Helping at Home_____bāng-máng zuò jiā-wù 帮忙做家务

We **have to** *shovel* the <u>snow</u>.
wǒ-mén **bì-xū** *chǎn* <u>xuě</u>
我 们 必 须 铲 雪。

Help me *mow the lawn.*
bāng wǒ *gē-cǎo*
帮 我 割 草。

Plant the *seeds* in <u>rows</u>.
bǎ *zhǒng-zi* **zhòng** chéng <u>háng</u>
把 种 子 种 成 行。

There are so *many* <u>weeds</u>!
zhè-me *duō* <u>zá-cǎo</u>
这 么 多 杂 草!

We **have** to *weed* the <u>garden</u>.
wǒ-mén **bì-xū** gěi <u>huā-yuán</u> *chú cǎo*
我 们 必 须 给 花 园 除 草。

Don't *dig* <u>too</u> much.
bié *wā* <u>tài</u> duō
别 挖 太 多。

Dig here in the <u>flowerbed</u>.
zài <u>huā-pǔ</u> lǐ *wā*
在 花 圃 里 挖。

Will you **help** me <u>water the flowers</u>?
nǐ néng **bāng** wǒ jiāo huā ma
你 能 帮 我 浇 花 吗?

Watch out for the <u>caterpillars</u>!
xiǎo-xīn <u>máo-mao-chóng</u>
小 心 毛 毛 虫!

Can you *rake* the <u>leaves</u>?
nǐ **néng** *qīng-lǐ* <u>luò-yè</u> ma
你 能 清 理 落 叶 吗?

qīng = clean, clear, rake

Throw the *leaves* into the/ <u>garbage</u> can/ <u>garbage</u> bag/.
bǎ *luò-yè* **rēng** dào/ <u>lā-jī</u>-tǒng lǐ / <u>lā-jī</u>-dài lǐ/
把 落 叶 扔 到/ 垃 圾 桶 里 / 垃 圾 袋 里/。

lǐ = into, inside

Put the *sprinkler*/ over <u>there</u>/ <u>here</u>/.
bǎ *jiāo-shuǐ-qì* **fàng** zài/ <u>nà-er</u>/ <u>zhè-er</u>/
把 浇 水 器 放 在/ 那 儿/ 这 儿/。

jiāo= to water

You can *prune* the <u>trees</u> in the **yard**.
nǐ néng gěi **yuàn-zi** lǐ de <u>shù</u> *jiǎn zhī*
你 能 给 院 子 里 的 树 剪 枝。

It's *too* <u>dangerous</u>.
tài <u>wēi-xiǎn</u> le
太 危 险 了。

We'll **build** a <u>wagon</u>.
wǒ-mén **zuò** yí-liàng <u>xiǎo-chē</u>
我 们 做 一 辆 小 车。

zuò yí-liàng = make (a vehicle)

Hit this *nail* with the <u>hammer</u>.
yòng <u>láng-tóu</u> *dìng* <u>dīng-zi</u>
用 榔 头 钉 钉 子。

Can you <u>sand</u> *this piece* of **wood**?
nǐ néng yòng <u>shā-zhǐ</u> *mó-guāng* *zhè-kuài* **mù-tóu** ma
你 能 用 砂 纸 磨 光 这 块 木 头 吗?

shā-zhǐ = sand paper; mó-guāng = polish

Saw *this* <u>board</u> in two.
bǎ *zhè-kuài* <u>bǎn-zi</u> **jù** chéng liǎng kuài
把 这 块 板 子 锯 成 两 块。

Do you **want** to *watch*?
nǐ **xiǎng** *kàn* ma
你 想 看 吗?

Help me/ *repair*/ work on/ the <u>car</u>.
bāng wǒ *xiū-lǐ* <u>chē</u>
帮 我 修 理 车。

Wash the <u>car</u>.
xǐ <u>chē</u>
洗 车.

Vacuum the <u>car</u>.
gěi <u>chē</u> *xī-chén*
给 车 吸 尘 。

Sweep the <u>sidewalk</u> **clean**.
bǎ <u>rén-xíng-dào</u> **sǎo gān-jìng**
把 人 行 道 扫 干 净 。

Help me *hook up(set up)* the <u>computer</u>.
bāng wǒ bǎ <u>diàn-nǎo</u> *ān hǎo*
帮 我 把 电 脑 安 好 。
ān hǎo = set up (a machine)

I **need** your <u>help</u>.
wǒ **xū-yào** nǐ <u>bāng-máng</u>
我 需 要 你 帮 忙 。

Experience is the best teacher.   jīng-yàn shì zuì-hǎo de lǎo-shī

经 验 是 最 好 的 老 师

School at Home   jiā jiào 家 教

A popular trend is taking place in America where many children and parents are taking charge of their own education. They are doing this at home. For those children learning at home these sentences will be useful.

I can read myself! wǒ néng zì-jǐ dú-shū 我 能 自 己 读 书!

The **school bus** *just* went by!
xiào-chē *gāng-gāng* kāi guò-qù

校 车 刚 刚 开 过 去!

Time for us to *start*, too.
wǒ-mén yě gāi *kāi-shǐ* le

我 们 也 该 开 始 了。

gāi = should, ought

Where did we stop yesterday?
zuó-tiān wǒ-mén jiǎng dào **nǎ-er** le

昨 天 我 们 讲 到 哪 了?

jiǎng = talk

67

I'm **glad** we're *home* today.
Wǒ hěn **gāo-xìng** wǒ-mén jīn-tiān zài-jiā
我 很 高 兴 我 们 今 天 在 家。

We will **need** *paper* and pens.
wǒ-mén **xū-yào** *zhǐ* hé bǐ
我 们 需 要 纸 和 笔。

There are no staples.
méi-yǒu dìng-shū-dīng le
没 有 订 书 钉 了。

Do we **have to** do *math*?
wǒ-mén **bì-xū** zuò *shù-xué* tí ma
我 们 必 须 做 数 学 题 吗?

tí = (math) questions

Show (Teach) your sister how to do her math (*homework*).
jiāo nǐ mèi-mei zuò shù-xué tí (*zuò-yè*)
教 你 妹 妹 做 数 学 题 (作 业)。

You can **read** *while* I work with your brother.
wǒ bāng nǐ dì-di de *shí-hòu*, nǐ xiān zì-jǐ **dú**
我 帮 你 弟 弟 的 时 候,你 先 自 己 读。

Do you **want** to *ask* a question?
nǐ **xiǎng** *wèn* wèn-tí ma
你 想 问 问 题 吗?

Let's take a break and relax.
wǒ-mén xiū-xī yī-xià
我 们 休 息 一 下。

We'll **work** in the <u>garden</u>.
wǒ-mén dào <u>huā-yuán</u> lǐ **gàn-huó-er**
我 们 到 花 园 里 干 活 儿。

When we <u>come back</u>:
wǒ-mén <u>huí-lái</u> hòu
我 们 回 来 后：

we'll <u>e-mail</u> our *friend*,
gěi *péng-yǒu* fā <u>diàn-zǐ yóu-jiàn</u>
给 朋 友 发 电 子 邮 件，

fā = send; diàn-zǐ = electronic; yóu-jiàn = mail; gěi = for

we'll <u>read</u>,
dú-shū
读 书，

go on-line,
shàng-wǎng
上 网，

wǎng = net

we'll **paint** a *picture* for <u>Daddy</u>,
gěi <u>bà-ba</u> **huà** yí-zhāng *huà*
给 爸 爸 画 一 张 画，

we'll **bake** *cookies* for <u>Uncle Peter</u>.
gěi <u>bǐ-dé shū-shu</u> **zuò** *bǐng-gān*
给 彼 得 叔 叔 做 饼 干。

bǐ-dé = Peter; shū-shu = uncle (younger)

I'm **glad** we *don't have* any <u>exams</u>.
wǒ hěn **gāo-xìng** wǒ-mén *méi-yǒu* <u>kǎo-shì</u>
我 很 高 兴 我 们 没 有 考 试。

We **have** to <u>study</u>.
wǒ-mén **bì-xū** <u>dú-shū</u>
我 们 必 须 读 书。

Let's <u>practice</u>!
ràng wǒ-mén <u>liàn-xí</u>
让 我 们 练 习！

You've **got to** *learn* <u>that</u>.
nǐ **bì-xū** *xué-huì* <u>nà-ge</u>
你 必 须 学 会 那 个。

Let's skip *history* <u>today</u>!
<u>jīn-tiān</u> bù xué *lì-shǐ* le
今 天 不 学 历 史 了!

bù xué = not study

I **need** extra *time* for my <u>music</u>.
wǒ **xū-yào** duō yì-diǎn-er *shí-jiān* xué <u>yīn-yuè</u>
我 需 要 多 一 点 儿 时 间 学 音 乐。

duō = more, many; xué = study

My **crayons** are <u>missing</u>.
wǒ-de **là-bǐ** <u>diū le</u>
我 的 蜡 笔 丢 了。

Has anyone *seen* <u>them</u>?
yǒu rén *kàn-jiàn* <u>tā-mén</u> ma
有 人 看 见 它 们 吗?

You have <u>worked a lot</u>.
nǐ hěn <u>yòng-gōng</u>
你 很 用 功。

You have learned <u>something</u> *nice*.
nǐ xué huì le yì-xiē *hěn-hǎo* de <u>dōng-xi</u>
你 学 会 了 一 些 很 好 的 东西。

The **lesson** is/ *easy*/ <u>difficult</u>/.
zhè jié **kè** hěn/ *róng-yì* /<u>nán</u> /
这 节 课 很/ 容 易/ 难。

<u>Clean up</u> *everything*!
bǎ *dōng-xi* <u>shōu-shi gān-jìng</u>
把 东 西 收 拾 干 净!

Throw the *trash* in the <u>wastebasket</u>.
bǎ *fèi-wù* **rēng** dào <u>fèi-zhǐ-lǒu</u> lǐ
把 废 物 扔 到 废 纸 篓 里。

I **can** *read* <u>myself</u>!
wǒ **néng** <u>zì-jǐ</u> *dú-shū*
我 能 自 己 读 书!

Actions Speak Louder Than Words.

xíng-dòng shèng yú kōng-huà
行 动 胜 于 空 话。

Words of Praise

zàn-yáng 赞 扬

All the ways to say, "You're tops!" "Wonderful, wonderful, you!"
and many, many more words of praise. Use this chapter *often*.
You and your child will love it!

You make me happy!   nǐ zhēn jiào wǒ gāo-xìng
你 真 叫 我 高 兴!

What a beautiful <u>voice</u>!
nǐ-de <u>shēng-yīn</u> zhēn hǎo-tīng
你的 声 音 真 好 听!
hǎo-tīng = beautiful sound

You / walk / draw / speak / sing / dance / well.
Nǐ / zǒu-lù / huà-huà / shuō-huà / chàng-gē / tiào-wǔ / hǎo
你 / 走 路 / 画 画 / 说 话 / 唱 歌 / 跳 舞 / 好。

Words of Praise_____ zàn-yáng 赞 扬

How well you/ eat / write / swim / play/!
nǐ/ chī-fàn / xiě-zì / yóu-yǒng / yùn-dòng / zhēn hǎo/
你 / 吃饭 / 写字 / 游 泳 / 运 动 / 真 好/!
yùn-dòng = exercise, sports

You're <u>wonderful</u>!
nǐ hěn <u>bàng</u>
你 很 棒!
bang = excellent

You're a <u>genius</u>!
nǐ shì yí-gè <u>tiān-cái</u>
你 是 一 个 天 才!

How/ **nice**/ <u>cute</u>/ you are.
nǐ zhēn/ **hǎo**/ <u>kě-ài</u>/
你 真/ 好/ 可 爱/。
zhēn = really

How <u>handsome</u> you are!
nǐ zhēn <u>hǎo-kàn</u>
你 真 好 看!
zhēn = really

How <u>brave</u> you are!
nǐ zhēn <u>yǒng-gǎn</u>
你 真 勇 敢!

How <u>strong</u> you are!
ni zhēn <u>zhuàng</u>
你 真 壮!

This outfit <u>suits</u> you well.
zhè tào yī-fu <u>shì-hé</u> nǐ
这 套 衣 服 适 合 你。
yī-fu = cloth

What **pretty** <u>curls</u>.
hǎo **piào-liàng** de <u>juǎn-fà</u>
好 漂 亮 的 卷 发。

What <u>pretty</u> **eyes** you have.
nǐ-de **yǎn-jīng** zhēn <u>hǎo-kàn</u>
你 的 眼 睛 真 好 看。

72

I love your / eyes / hands / tummy/.
wǒ xǐ-huān nī-de/ yǎn-jīng / shǒu / xiǎo dù-zi/
我 喜 欢 你 的/ 眼 睛 / 手 / 小 肚 子/。

You are generous.
nǐ hěn dà-fāng
你 很 大 方。

I am **very** *thankful* for your help.
wǒ **fēi-cháng** *gǎn-xiè* nǐ bāng-máng
我 非 常 感 谢 你 帮 忙。

I like you (**very much**).
wǒ (**fēi-cháng**) xǐ-huān nǐ
我 (非 常) 喜 欢 你。

I love you.
wǒ ài nǐ
我 爱 你。

Bravo!
hǎo-à
好 啊!

Well done!
hěn bàng
很 棒!
bàng = excellent

Encore!
zài lái yí-gè
再 来 一 个!

I like the way you play **quietly** by *yourself.*
wǒ xǐ-huān *nǐ zì-jǐ* **ān-jìng-de** wán
我 喜 欢 你 自 己 安 静 地 玩。

Try *again*! (one time)
zài **shì** yí-cì
再 试 一 次!

Don't give up!
bié fàng-qì
别 放 弃!

I (don't) <u>understand</u>.
wǒ (bù) <u>míng-bái</u>
我 (不) 明 白。

What does it mean?
zhè shì shén-me yì-si
这 是 什 么 意 思?

What a great <u>idea</u>!
hǎo <u>zhú-yì</u>
好 主 意!

You're getting <u>better</u> and <u>better</u>.
nǐ <u>yuè lái yuè hǎo</u> le
你 越 来 越 好 了。
le – change of state

That's sweet of you to <u>help</u>.
nǐ néng <u>bāng-máng</u> zhēn hǎo
你 能 帮 忙 真 好。

You **cleaned** your <u>room</u>!
nǐ <u>dǎ-sǎo</u> le nǐ-de <u>fáng-jiān</u>
你 打 扫 了 你 的 房 间!

You **should** be <u>proud</u> of yourself.
ni **yīng-gāi** <u>zì-háo</u>
你 应 该 自 豪。

You are (**handy**) **good** with your <u>hands</u>.
nǐ-de <u>shǒu</u> hěn **qiǎo**
你 的 手 很 巧。
qiǎo = skillful, handy

You make me <u>happy</u>!
nǐ zhēn jiào wǒ <u>gāo-xìng</u>
你 真 叫 我 高 兴!
jiào = call, be called

Clothes Make the Man.

rén kào yī zhuāng
人 靠 衣 装。

Shopping

mǎi dōng-xī 买东西

Shopping offers many opportunities to learn and use new vocabulary: food, drinks, clothing, toys, tools, shops, colors. Many more vocabulary groups can be found in the Vocabulary section of this book.

Let's go shopping! wǒ-mén mǎi dōng-xī qù
我 们 买 东 西 去!

Do you want to <u>go shopping</u>?
nǐ xiǎng <u>qù mǎi dōng-xī</u> ma
你 想 去 买 东 西 吗?

I **have to** <u>write</u> a shopping *list*.
wǒ **bì-xū** <u>xiě</u> gòu-wù *dān*
我 必 须 写 购 物 单。
gòu-wù = shopping

Do you <u>want</u> to go with me?
nǐ <u>xiǎng</u> gēn wǒ qù ma
你 想 跟 我 去 吗?

Go *with* me to:
gēn wǒ <u>qù</u>:
跟 我 去:

75

lumber yard,
mù-cái chǎng
木 材 场

hardware store,
wǔ-jīn diàn
五 金 店

book store,
shū-diàn
书 店

nursery,
miáo-pǔ
苗 圃

gas station,
jiā-yóu-zhàn
加 油 站

toy store,
wán-jù diàn
玩 具 店

barber,
lǐ-fà diàn
理 发 店
lǐ-fà = cut hair

bakery,
miàn-bāo diàn
面 包 店
miàn-bāo = bread

grocery store,
cài diàn
菜 店

laundromat,
xǐ-yī diàn
洗 衣 店
xǐ-yī = washing cloth

sports store,
tǐ-yù yòng-pǐn diàn
体 育 用 品 店

delicatessen
shú-shí diàn
熟 食 店
shú-shí = cooked food

department store,
shāng-diàn
商 店
shāng = merchandise

mall,
shāng-chǎng
商 场

video store.
lù-yǐng-dài diàn
录 影 带 店.
lù-yǐng-dài = video tape

I am **going** to the supermarket.
wǒ yào **qù** chāo-shì
我 要 去 超 市。

I have to **buy**…
wǒ bì-xū **mǎi**…
我 必 须 买……

76

I **must** return (bring something back)…
wŏ **bì-xū** tuì huò …
我 必 须 退 货...
　　　　tuì huò = return merchandise

There's a sale.
yŏu jiăn jià shāng-pĭn
有 减 价 商 品。

What would you like to go buy?
nĭ xiăng măi *shén-me*
你 想 买 什 么?

Let's take the/ **elevator**/ escalator/?
zuò/ **diàn-tī**/ zì-dòng lóu-tī/
坐/ 电 梯 /自 动 楼 梯/?

You can/ **sit**/ stay/ in the *shopping cart*.
nĭ néng/ **zuò** zài/ dāi zài/ *gòu-wù chē* li
你 能 / 坐 在/ 呆 在/ 购 物 车 里。

Place your **feet** through the openings.
bă nĭ-de **jiăo** cóng kòng-dāng chuān guò-qù
把 你 的 脚 从 空 档 穿 过 去。

Can I help you?
nín *xiăng yào* shén-me
您 想 要 什 么?
xiăng yào= want to have (what)

I'd **like** to have...(something)
wŏ **xiăng** yào…
我 想 要……

We cannot **spend** *too much* <u>money</u>.
wǒ-mén bù-néng **huā** *tài-duō* <u>qián</u>
我 们 不 能 花 太 多 钱。

How much *money* do you <u>have</u>?
nǐ <u>yǒu</u> **duō-shǎo** *qián*
你 有 多 少 钱？

We **cannot** *buy* <u>that</u>.
wǒ-mén **bù-néng** *mǎi* <u>nà-ge</u>
我 们 不 能 买 那 个。

I'm somewhat **short of** <u>money</u>.
wǒ-de <u>qián</u> **bú-gòu**
我 的 钱 不 够。
bú-gòu = not enough

I do **not have** any <u>money</u>.
wǒ **méi** dài <u>qián</u>
我 没 带 钱。
dài = bring

That's **too** <u>expensive</u>.
tài <u>guì</u> le
太 贵 了。

Perhaps (*buy*) something <u>cheaper</u>.
yě-xǔ *mǎi* <u>pián-yi-diǎn-er de</u>
也 许 买 便 宜 点 儿 的。

I **need** *some* <u>money</u>.
wǒ **xū-yào** *yì-xiē* <u>qián</u>
我 需 要 一 些 钱。

That's/ **a good buy**/ <u>on sale</u>/.
<u>nà-ge</u> / **hěn huá-suàn**/ <u>jiǎn-jià</u>/
那 个/ 很 划 算/ 减 价/。

How much (<u>money</u>)is it?
duō-shǎo <u>qián</u>
多 少 钱？

The **clerk** is <u>over there</u>.
shòu-huò-yuán zài <u>nà-biān</u>
售 货 员 在 那 边。

Should we <u>buy</u> it?
wǒ-mén <u>mǎi-bù-mǎi</u>
我 们 买 不 买?

<u>Try</u> it *on*.
chuān shàng <u>shì-shi</u>
穿 上 试 试。

What size is this <u>coat</u>?
zhè jiàn <u>wài-tào</u> duó dà **hào**
这 件 外 套 多 大 号?

jiàn = MW – piece; duó dà = how big; hào = size or number

This is **too**/ *tight*/ <u>loose</u>/.
tài/ *jǐn*/ <u>sōng</u>/
太/ 紧 / 松/。

Let me <u>see</u> that.
ràng wǒ <u>kàn-kan</u> nà jiàn
让 我 看 看 那 件。

This is **too**/ *large*/ <u>small</u>/ for you.
zhè jiàn nǐ chuān **tài**/ *dà*/ <u>xiǎo</u>/
这 件 你 穿 太/ 大/ 小/。

jiàn – MW – piece; chuān = wear (clothes)

Come over here, <u>please</u>.
qǐng dào zhè-biān **lái**
请 到 这 边 来。

dào = arrive, go to

We'll <u>meet</u> *here* in **an hour**.
yì xiǎo-shí hòu <u>zài</u> *zhè* pèng-miàn
一 小 时 后 在 这 碰 面。

That will cost *four* <u>yuan</u>.
sì kuài <u>rén-mín-bì</u>
4 块 人 民 币。
rén-mín-bì = Chinese currency

Count your <u>change</u>.
shǔ-shǔ nǐ-de <u>líng-qián</u>
数 数 你 的 零 钱。

Don't <u>touch</u> that.
bié <u>pèng</u> nà-ge
别 碰 那 个。

How do I <u>get to</u> (place)?
qù (place) **zěn-me** <u>zǒu</u>
去 (place) 怎 么 走?

79

Stay with/ me/ Mom/ Dad/.
bié lí-kāi/ wǒ/ mā-ma/ bà-ba/
别 离 开/ 我/ 妈 妈/ 爸 爸/。
bié lí-kāi = don't leave

Do you **have** a shopping bag?
nǐ **yǒu** gòu-wù-dài ma
你 有 购 物 袋 吗?

Do you **think** *Dad* would like it?
nǐ **jué-de** *bà-ba* huì xǐ-huān zhè-ge ma
你 觉 得 爸 爸 会 喜 欢 这 个 吗?
jué-de = think, feel

The **aisles** are crowded.
tōng-dào hén jǐ
通 道 很 挤。

Where is/ the cashier/ check out/?
/shōu-yín-yuán/ fù-zhàng-kǒu/ zài nǎ-er
/ 收 银 员 / 付 帐 口/ 在 哪 儿?

Where's the restroom?
cè-suǒ zài nǎ-er
厕 所 在 哪 儿?

We **can** go window-shopping.
wǒ-mén **kě-yǐ** liú-liǎn chú-chuāng
我 们 可 以 浏 览 橱 窗。

The/ exit/entrance/ is over there.
/chū-kǒu/ jìn-kǒu/ zài nà-biān
/出 口/ 进 口 / 在 那 边。

We're looking for/ toys/ furniture/ clothing/.
wǒ-mén zhǎo/ wán-jù/ jiā-jù / yī-fu/
我 们 找 / 玩 具/ 家 俱/ 衣 服/。

No *parking*!
jìn-zhǐ *tíng-chē*
禁 止 停 车!
jìn-zhǐ = forbid

Let's go shopping!
wǒ-mén mǎi dōng-xī qù
我 们 买 东 西 去!

80

Work while you work; play while you play
zhuān-xīn zuò-shì, jìn-qíng wán-shuǎ
专 心 做 事，尽 情 玩 耍。

Fun!   Yú-lè 娱乐!

If this chapter's pages don't have paint stains, water marks, tire tracks and gum sticking the pages together, you're not getting all there is to wring from these pages! Be sure to write down additional sentences and expressions you've learned elsewhere that are appropriate.

Have fun!   hǎo-hāo wán 好好玩!

You/ **may**/ <u>can</u>:   **play** in the <u>yard</u>,
nǐ/ **kě-yǐ**/ <u>néng</u>   zài <u>yuàn-zi</u> lǐ **wán**
你/ 可以/ 能: 在 院 子 里玩,

go to the <u>playground</u>,   **go** to the (soccer, baseball) <u>field</u>,
qù <u>yóu-xì-chǎng</u>   **qù** (zú-qiú, bàng-qiú) <u>chǎng</u>
去 游 戏 场,   去 (足 球, 棒 球) 场,

  go to your *friend*'s <u>house</u> to play   doctor <u>and</u> nurse,
  qù *péng-yǒu* jiā wán   yī-shēng <u>hé</u> hù-shì
  去 朋 友 家 玩   医 生 和 护 士,

Fun!_____ yú-lè 娱乐!

store,   with the computer,   hide and seek.
shāng-diàn   diàn-nǎo   zhuō-mí-cáng
商　店,   电　脑,   捉　迷　藏.

Can I? (Is it allowed...?)   Is it OK? Can I...?
kě-yǐ ma   ...xíng ma
可 以 吗？   ... 行　吗？

May I <u>play</u> with you?   Do you **want** to <u>play</u> with me?
wǒ **kě-yǐ** hé nǐ <u>wán</u> ma   nǐ **xiǎng** hé wǒ <u>wán</u> ma
我 可 以 和 你 玩 吗?   你 想 和 我 玩 吗?

                (Airplanes)   (fēi-jī　飞 机)

Pilot *to* <u>control tower</u>.   **Please** *fasten* your <u>seatbelts</u>.
jiào-shǐ-yuán *duì* <u>kòng-zhì-tái</u> **qǐng** *jì shàng* <u>ān-quán-dài</u>
驾 驶 员 对 控 制 台。   请 系 上 安 全 带。

I'm <u>taking off</u>.   **Throttle** <u>down</u>!
wǒ jiù yào <u>qǐ-fēi</u>   <u>fàng-xià</u> **jié-liú-gān**
我 就 要 起飞。   放 下 节 流 杆!

Clear the <u>runway</u>!   On **which** <u>runway</u> may we *land*?
qīng-lǐ <u>pǎo-dào</u>   wǒ-mén zài **nǎ**-tiáo <u>pǎo-dào</u> *jiàng-luò*
清 理 跑 道!   我 们 在 哪 条 跑 道 降 落?

We're running out of fuel!
wǒ-mén kuài méi yóu le
我 们 快 没 油 了!

My **plane** *can* do a <u>loop</u>.
wǒ-de **fēi-jī** *néng* zhuàn yī-<u>quān</u>
我 的 飞 机 能 转 一 圈。

I **worked** three *weeks* on my <u>model</u>.
wǒ huā-le sān-gè *xīng-qī* **zuò** wǒ-de <u>mó-xíng</u>
我 花 了 三 个 星 期 做 我 的 模 型。

How long is the **flight** to <u>China</u>?
fēi <u>zhōng-guó</u> yào *duō-cháng shí-jiān*
飞 中 国 要 多 长 时 间?

(In the Garden)   (zài huā-yuán lǐ   在花园里)

Go/ outside/ inside/ and <u>play</u>.
dào/ wài-biān/ lǐ-biān/ <u>wán</u>
到 / 外 边/ 里 边/ 玩。

<u>Play</u>/ in the yard/ in the sand box/.
/zài yuàn-zi lǐ/ zài shā-xiāng lǐ / <u>wán</u>
/ 在 院 子里/ 在 沙 箱 里 / 玩。

Do you **want** to *blow* <u>soap</u> bubbles?
nǐ **xiǎng** *chuī* <u>féi-zào</u> pào ma
你 想 吹 肥皂 泡 吗?
pào = bubbles

Don't <u>play</u> in the *dirt*.
bié zài *tǔ-dì shàng* <u>wán</u>
别 在 土 地 上 玩。
tǔ = dirt, dust; dì = land

Please don't *pick* the <u>flowers</u>!
qǐng bú-yào *zhāi* <u>huā</u>
请 不 要 摘 花!

You **can** *swim* in the <u>pool</u> if I am with you.
rú-guǒ wǒ-hé-nǐ zài-yī-qǐ, nǐ **néng** zài <u>yóu-yǒng-chí</u> lǐ *yóu-yǒng*
如 果 我 和 你 在 一 起, 你 能 在 游 泳 池 里 游 泳。
rú-guǒ = if; yī-qǐ = together

<u>Jump off</u> the **diving board** as I have shown you.
zhào wǒ-de yàng-zi cóng **tiào-shuǐ-bǎn** shàng <u>tiào-xià-lái</u>
照 我 的 样 子 从 跳 水 板 上 跳 下 来。
yàng-zi = the way one appears

Be **careful** *when* you are <u>climbing the tree</u>.
<u>pá-shù</u> de *shí-hòu* **xiǎo-xīn**
爬 树 的 时 候 小 心。

Both of you *can* sit in the <u>wagon</u>.
nǐ-mén **liǎng-gè dōu** *néng* zuò zài <u>xiǎo-chē</u> lǐ
你 们 两 个 都 能 坐 在 小 车 里。

There's *enough* <u>room</u> for **two**.
yǒu *zú-gòu* de <u>dì-fāng</u> zuò **liǎng-gè** rén
有 足 够 的 地 方 坐 两 个 人。

Sweep up the <u>glass</u>.
bǎ <u>bō-li</u> **sǎo** gān-jìng
把 玻璃 扫 干 净。

Can you *replace* the broken <u>(glass)</u>?
nǐ **néng** *huàn* xīn <u>bō-li</u> ma
你 能 换 新 玻 璃 吗?

Don't **leave** the <u>yard</u>.
bié **lí-kāi** <u>yuàn-zi</u>
别离开 院 子。

(Baseball)   (bàng-qiú 棒球)

It's your turn. (at bat, hit the ball)
gāi nǐ (jī-qiú) le
该 你 (击球) 了。
gāi = should; jī-qiú = hit the ball

Catch/ *Throw*/ the <u>ball</u>.
jiē/ *rēng*/ <u>qiú</u>
接/ 扔 / 球。

(<u>Put</u>) Hold the **bat** *behind you.*
bǎ **qiú-bàng** <u>fàng</u> zài *shēn-hòu*
把 球 棒 放 在 身 后。

<u>Keep your eye on</u> the **ball**!
<u>dīng-zhù</u> **qiú**
盯 住 球!

Swing with the bat.
huī-bàng
挥 棒。

You <u>missed</u> the *ball*.
<u>méi dǎ-zháo</u> *qiú*
没 打 着 球。
dǎ = hit

Score a <u>run</u>!
pǎo yī-quān **dé-fēn**
跑 一 圈 得 分!

You <u>hit the ball</u> very well.
nǐ <u>jī-qiú</u> hěn-hǎo
你击 球 很 好。

85

Fun!_____ yú-lè 娱乐!

(Bicycling)   (qí jiǎo-tà-chē 骑 脚 踏 车)

Put your <u>feet</u> on the *pedals*.
bǎ <u>jiǎo</u> **fàng** zài *tà-bǎn* shàng
把 脚 放 在 踏 板 上。

Don't *pedal* so <u>hard</u>.
bié zhè-me <u>yòng-lì</u> *cǎi tà-bǎn*
别 这 么 用 力 踩 踏 板。
yòng-lì = use strength

Keep pedaling.
jì-xù cǎi <u>tà-bǎn</u>
继 续 踩 踏 板。
tà-bǎn = pedal; cǎi = step on

I've <u>got a hold</u> of you.
wǒ <u>fú-zhe</u> nǐ ne
我 扶 着 你 呢。

Try to *keep* your <u>balance</u>.
jìn-liàng *bǎo-chí* <u>píng-héng</u>
尽 量 保 持 平 衡。

Let me <u>try</u>!
ràng wǒ <u>shì-shi</u>
让 我 试 试!

Hold on to the <u>handlebars</u>.
zhuā-zhù <u>bǎ-shǒu</u>
抓 住 把 手。

Turn/ to the <u>right</u>/ to the *left*/.
yòu-zhuǎn/ *zuǒ-zhuǎn*
右 转/ 左 转。

Go <u>straight</u>.
<u>zhí</u> **zǒu**
直 走。

You're <u>riding your bicycle</u> very well.
nǐ <u>qí-chē</u> hěn-hǎo
你 骑 车 很 好。

Don't <u>ride your bicycle</u> *in the street*. There is <u>too much</u> traffic/*cars*.
bié *zài mǎ-lù shàng* <u>qí-chē</u>   *chē* <u>tài-duō</u> le
别 在 马 路 上 骑 车。   车 太 多 了。

86

You're **going** <u>too fast</u>!
nǐ **qí-de** <u>tài-kuài</u> le
你 骑 得 太 快 了!

Put on the brakes!
shā-chē
刹 车!

shā-chē = brakes

You **need** to put on your <u>helmet</u>!
nǐ **xū-yào** dài <u>ān-quán-mào</u>
你需要 戴安全 帽!

(Board Games)   (xià-qí 下 棋)

Do you **want** to play/ *checkers*/ <u>chess</u>/ ?
nǐ **xiǎng** xià/ *tiào qí*/ <u>xiàng-qí</u>/ ma
你 想 下/ 跳 棋/ 象 棋/ 吗?

qí is for all board games

Whose turn is it?
gāi shuí le
该 谁 了?

gāi = should; shuí = who

It's my turn.
gāi wǒ le
该 我 了。

It's your turn.
gāi nǐ le
该 你 了。

I'll <u>throw</u> the *dice* (now).
(xiàn-zài) wǒ yào <u>rēng</u> *shǎi-zī* le
(现 在) 我 要 扔 色子 了。

I **want** the *blue* figure (<u>piece</u>).
wǒ **xiǎng** yào *lán* <u>qí</u>
我 想 要 蓝 棋。

Your <u>piece</u> is in the **wrong** place.
nǐ-de <u>qí</u> fàng **cuò** le
你的 棋 放 错 了。

Place it <u>on</u> the *right* spot.
bǎ tā **fàng** *duì*
把它 放 对。

duì= correct, right

You aren't **playing** <u>fairly</u>.
nǐ **wán** de bù <u>gōng-píng</u>
你 玩 得 不 公 平。

You **have to** <u>pay</u> me *money*.
nǐ **bì-xū** <u>fù</u> wǒ *qián*
你 必 须 付 我 钱。

Move/ *forwards*/ <u>backwards</u>/.
wǎng/ *qiǎn*/ <u>hòu</u> /
往 / 前/ 后/。

You have/ **won**/ <u>lost</u>/.
nǐ/ **yíng-le**/ <u>shū-le</u>/
你/ 赢 了/ 输 了/。

(Boats)   (chuán 船)

All aboard!
shàng-chuán-le
上 船 了!

We're **leaving** the <u>port</u>.
wǒ-mén zhèng-zài **lí-kāi** <u>gǎng-kǒu</u>
我 们 正 在 离 开 港 口。
zhèng-zài = in the middle of

We're sailing to <u>China</u>.
wǒ-mén kāi wǎng <u>zhōng-guó</u>
我 们 开 往 中 国。
kāi = operate, drive; wǎng = in the direction of

The **boat** is <u>sinking</u>.
chuán yào <u>chén-le</u>
船 要 沉 了。
yào = about to

Man <u>overboard</u>!
yǒu-**rén** <u>luò-shuǐ</u>
有 人 落 水!

Lower the <u>life boats</u>!
bǎ <u>jiù-shēng-chuán</u> **fàng-xià-qù**
把 救 生 船 放 下 去!

Abandon <u>ship</u>!
qì-<u>chuán</u>
弃 船!

Fun!_____ yú-lè 娱乐!

We're **going**/ boating/ kayaking/.
wǒ-mén **qù**/ huá-chuán/ huá dú-mù-zhōu/
我 们 去/ 划 船 / 划 独木 舟。

Slow down!
fàng-màn
放 慢!

I'll drive.
wǒ lái kāi
我 来 开。

You **can** water-ski.
nǐ **néng** huá-shuǐ
你 能 滑 水。

Get out and push!
chū-qù tuī
出 去 推!

Get the oars!
bǎ jiǎng **ná**-lái
把 桨 拿 来!

I'll paddle.
wǒ lái huá
我 来 划。

(Camping)   (lù-yíng 露营)

How long do we *want* to camp?
wǒ-mén *xiǎng* lù-yíng **duō-jiǔ**
我 们 想 露 营 多 久?

We **need** a *new* tent.
wǒ-mén **xū-yào** yí-gè *xīn* zhàng-péng
我 们 需 要 一个 新 帐 篷。

This one has **holes** in it.
zhè shàng-miàn yǒu **dòng**
这 上 面 有 洞。

I am **happy** that we *still have* our camper.
wǒ hěn **gāo-xìng** wǒ-mén *hái-yǒu* lù-yíng-chē
我 很 高 兴 我 们 还 有 露 营 车。

Let's <u>pitch</u> the **tent** (*together*).
wǒ-mén (*yì-qǐ*) <u>dā</u>-**zhàng-péng**
我 们 (一起) 搭 帐 篷。
dā = set up, build

I want to **camp** *right by* the <u>lake</u>.
wǒ xiǎng *jiù zài* <u>hú</u>-biān **lù-yíng**
我 想 就 在 湖 边 露 营。

Those who have a **sleeping bag** should *sleep* <u>outdoors</u>.
yǒu **shuì-dài** de rén yīng-gāi *shuì* <u>wài-biān</u>
有 睡 袋 的 人 应 该 睡 外 边。
yīng-gāi = should, ought

Set up the <u>stove</u>.
dā <u>lú-zi</u>
搭 炉子。
dā = set up, build

(Cars) (qì-chē 汽 车)

The **car** broke down.
chē huài-le
车 坏 了。
huài = broken

It (**car**) doesn't <u>move</u> any more.
chē bú-<u>dòng</u>-le
车 不 动 了。

Why <u>doesn't</u> the *car* <u>go</u>?
wèi-shén-me *chē* <u>bù-zǒu</u>
为 什 么 车 不 走?

Push the <u>car</u>!
tuī-chē
推 车!

Fill'er up!
jiā mǎn yóu
加 满 油!
jiā = add

90

Check the **oil**, *water*, battery!
jiǎn-chá jī-yóu, *shuǐ,* diàn-chí
检 查 机 油，水， 电 池！

Drive the *car* into the garage!
bǎ *chē* **kāi** dào chē-kù lǐ
把 车 开 到 车 库 里！
dào = up to

I like a pick-up!
wǒ xǐ-huān kǎ-chē
我 喜 欢 卡 车！

(**Color** and Paste) (**yán-sè** hé jiàng-hú 颜 色 和 浆 糊)

She **may** **use** the crayons.
tā **kě-yǐ** *yòng* là-bǐ
她可以 用 蜡笔。

Color the *sun* yellow.
gěi *tài-yáng* **tú-shàng** huáng-sè
给太 阳 涂 上 黄 色。

Color the *bird* the color you want.
gěi *niǎo* **tú-shàng** nǐ-yào-de yán-sè
给 鸟 涂 上 你 要 的 颜色。

Draw the / circle, /triangle, / rectangle/ and the square like this.
xiàng zhè-yàng **huà** /yuán-quān,/ sān-jiǎo,/ cháng-fāng-xíng/ hé/ sì-fāng-xíng/
像 这 样 画 / 圆 圈， / 三 角， / 长 方 形 / 和/ 四 方 形/。

Cut this *picture* out of the magazine.
bǎ zhè-zhāng *zhào-piān* cóng zá-zhì shàng **jiǎn** xià lái
把 这 张 照 片 从 杂 志 上 剪 下 来。

91

Paste it *carefully* onto the <u>paper</u>.
bǎ tā *xiǎo-xīn*-de **tiē-zài** <u>zhǐ</u> shàng
把 它 小 心 地 贴 在 纸 上。

Fold the <u>paper</u>.
bǎ <u>zhǐ</u> **zhé-qǐ-lái**
把 纸 折 起 来。

Don't *tear* the <u>paper</u>!
bié bǎ <u>zhǐ</u> *sī-pò* le
别 把 纸 撕 破 了!

Roll out the *clay* <u>like this</u>.
<u>xiàng zhè-yàng</u> **róu-kāi** *yóu-ní*
像 这 样 揉 开 油 泥。

Squeeze the *clay* <u>like this</u>.
<u>xiàng zhè-yàng</u> **niē** *yóu-ní*
像 这 样 捏 油 泥。

Form the *clay* <u>like this</u>.
bǎ *yóu-ní* **zuò-chéng** <u>zhè-yàng</u>
把 油 泥 做 成 这 样。

(Computer)   (diàn-nǎo 电 脑)

Do you **want** to *play* a computer <u>game</u>?
nǐ **xiǎng** *wán* diàn-nǎo <u>yóu-xì</u> ma
你 想 玩 电 脑 游 戏 吗?

We'll **print** <u>that</u>.
wǒ-mén bǎ <u>nà-gè</u> **yìn-chū-lái**
我 们 把 那 个 印 出 来。

There's a <u>computer</u> *error*.
<u>diàn-nǎo</u> chū *wèn-tí* le
电 脑 出 问 题 了。
chū = occur; wèn-tí = error, problem

92

We'll go on-line.
wǒ-mén shàng wǎng
我 们 上 网。
wǎng = web

(Dolls)　　(wá-wa 娃 娃)

What is your *doll*'s name?
nǐ-de *wá-wa* jiào **shén-me** mǐng-zì
你 的 娃 娃 叫 什 么 名 字?
jiào = call, is called

Feed the **doll**.
gěi **wá-wa** wèi-fàn
给 娃 娃 喂 饭。
gěi = give

Dress the **doll**.
gěi **wá-wa** chuān-yī-fu
给 娃 娃 穿 衣 服。
yī-fu = cloth

I **have to**/ brush/ comb/ her hair.
wǒ **bì-xū** gěi tā shū-tóu-fa
我 必 须 给 她 梳 头 发。

Put her *down* gently.
bǎ tā qīng-qīng **fàng** *xià-lái*
把 她 轻 轻 放 下 来。

Don't *drag* her on the floor.
bié zài dì-shàng *tuō* tā
别 在 地 上 拖 她。

Put your *dolls* **away**.
bǎ nǐ-de *wá-wa* **fàng yì-biān**
把 你 的 娃 娃 放 一 边。
yì-biān = one side

It's time for your doll to *sleep*.
nǐ-de wá-wa gāi *shuì-jiào* le
你 的 娃 娃 该 睡 觉 了。

Your doll is pretty.
nǐ-de wá-wa hěn hǎo-kàn
你 的 娃 娃 很 好 看。

93

(Guess what!)　　　(cāi-cāi kàn 猜 猜 看!)

I **sit** on water-lilies. I *say*, "Rip-it."?
wǒ **zuò**-zài hé-yè shàng. wǒ *shuō* "guá guá"
我 坐 在 荷 叶 上。 我 说: "呱 呱。"
shàng = on　　　　　I **catch** *insects* with my tongue.
　　　　　　　　　wǒ yòng shé-tóu **zhuā** *kūn-chóng*
　　　　　　　　　我 用 舌 头 抓 昆 虫。
What *animal* am I? (a frog)
wǒ shì **shén-me** *dòng-wù* (yì-zhī qīng-wā)
我 是 什 么 动 物? (一只 青 蛙)

I bark and **growl**. I *chase* cats. I say, "Ruff-ruff.")
wǒ wāng-wāng **jiào**. wǒ *zhuī* xiǎo-māo. wǒ shuō "wāng-wāng"
我 汪 汪 叫。我 追 小 猫。我 说: " 汪 汪。"
　　　　　　　　　What *animal* am I? (a dog)
　　　　　　　　　wǒ shì **shén-me** *dòng-wù* (yì-zhī gǒu)
　　　　　　　　　我 是 什 么 动 物? (一只 狗)

I **carry** my *baby* in my pouch.
wǒ bǎ wǒ-de *bǎo-bāo* **zhuāng** zài dù-dài lǐ
我 把 我 的 宝 宝 装 在 肚 袋里。
　　　　　I hop.
　　　　　wǒ tiào-yuè
　　　　　我 跳 跃。
　　　　　　What *animal* am I? (a kangaroo)
　　　　　wǒ shì **shén-me** *dòng-wù* (yì-zhī dài-shǒu)
　　　　　我 是 什 么 动 物? (一只 袋鼠)

I strut and <u>crow</u>. *(sound of rooster)*
wǒ áng-shǒu *wō-wō* <u>jiào</u>.
我 昂 首 喔 喔 叫。

áng-shǒu = raise head (proud)

I **awaken** people <u>early</u> on the farm. *(farm people)*
wǒ qīng-zǎo bǎ nóng-fū **jiào-xǐng**
我 清 早 把 农 夫 叫 醒。

What *animal* am I? (<u>a rooster</u>)
wǒ shì **shén-me** *dòng-wù* (yì-zhī <u>gōng-jī</u>)
我 是 什 么 动 物? (一只 公 鸡)

(On the <u>playground</u>) (zài <u>yóu-xì-chǎng</u> shàng 在 游 戏 场 上)

<u>Go</u> and <u>hide</u>!	Scram! (<u>fast</u>)	<u>Where</u> are you? <u>Where</u> am I?
qù <u>cáng-qǐ-lái</u>	kuài	nǐ zài <u>nǎ</u>? wǒ zài <u>nǎ</u>?
去 藏 起 来!	快!	你在哪? 我 在 哪?

kuài = quick, hurry

Swing! Don't *swing* <u>too high</u>.
dàng qiū-qiān. bié *dàng*-de <u>tài-gāo</u>
荡 秋 千! 别 荡 得 太 高。

I **can** *push* you <u>gently</u>!
wǒ **néng** qīng-qīng *tuī* nǐ
我 能 轻 轻 推 你。

Don't **jump** *off* the <u>swing</u>!
bié *cóng* qiū-qiān shàng **tiào-xià-lái**
别 从 秋 千 上 跳 下 来!

Don't **close** your <u>eyes</u>!
bié **bì-yǎn**
别 闭 眼!

bì = close (eyes, mouth)

Don't **stand on** the swing!
bié **zhàn-zài** qiū-qiān **shàng**
别 站 在 秋 千 上!

Slide *down* slowly!
màn-mān huá *xià-lái*
慢 慢 滑 下 来!

Hold on to/ the *slide*/ the merry-go-round/ tightly!
jǐn-jǐn zhuā-zhù/ *huá-tī*/ zhuàn-mǎ/
紧 紧 抓 住 / 滑 梯 / 转 马 / !

The **kite** is falling.
fēng-zhēng zài wǎng-xià-diào
风 筝 在 往 下 掉。
wǎng-xià-diào = to drop

There's *not enough* wind.
fēng *bú-gòu* dà
风 不 够 大。
dà = big

Hold the *kite*/ tightly/ loosely/.
zhuā-jǐn/ fàng-sōng/ *fēng-zhēng*/
抓 紧 / 放 松 / 风 筝 / 。
fàng-sōng = let loose

Do you **want** to jump rope?
nǐ **xiǎng** tiào-shéng ma
你 想 跳 绳 吗?

Shoot the *marbles* **into** the circle.
bǎ *tán-qiú* **tán jìn** quān lǐ
把 弹 球 弹 进 圈 里。

Blow up the balloon.
chuī qì-qiú
吹 气 球。

Air *is leaking* from the balloon!
qì-qiú *lòu-qì* le
气 球 漏 气 了!

Help! Fire!
jiù-mìng! zháo-huǒ le
救 命! 着 火 了!

96

Fun! _____ yú-lè 娱乐!

Call the *fire department*!　　Call 911!　　Sound the <u>siren</u>!
gěi *xiāo-fáng-duì* **dǎ-diàn-huà**　dǎ jiǔ yī yī　kāi <u>jǐng-dí</u>
给 消 防 队 打 电 话!　　打 9 1 1!　　开 警 笛!
　　　　　　　　　　　　　　　　　　　　　kāi = open, turn on

I'm the **leader**. <u>Follow me</u>.
wǒ shì **lǐng-duì**, <u>gēn-zhè-wǒ</u>
我 是 领 队，跟 着 我。
　　　gēn = with

My **skates** are <u>dull</u>.　　They (**should**) need to <u>be sharpened</u>.
wǒ-de **bīng-dāo** <u>dùn</u> le　　**gāi** <u>mó-dāo</u> le
我 的 冰 刀 钝 了。　　该 磨 刀 了。

Hold on to me. I'll help you <u>skate</u>.　**Push** with (*Use*) the <u>left foot</u>!
zhuā-zhè-wǒ wǒ dài nǐ <u>huá-bīng</u>　*yòng* <u>zuǒ-jiǎo</u> **dēng**
抓 着 我。我 带 你 滑 冰。　　用 左 脚 蹬!
dài = lead, carry

Lift the <u>right foot</u>!　　　　**Skate** *around* the <u>rink</u>.
tái <u>yòu-jiǎo</u>　　　　　　　*rào* <u>liū-bīng-chǎng</u> **huá**
抬 右 脚!　　　　　　　绕 溜 冰 场 滑。

You're ready to *skate* <u>backwards</u>.
nǐ néng <u>dào</u> *huá* le
你 能 倒 滑 了。

97

Run with the *ball*!
dài *qiú* **pǎo**
带 球 跑！
dài = carry (with hand or foot in soccer)

Shoot the ball into the goal!
shè-mén
射 门！

Don't **touch** the *ball* with your hands!
bié yòng shǒu **pèng** *qiú*
别 用 手 碰 球！
yòng = use

Get free! (Don't stand there!)
bié zhàn-zhe
别 站 着！
zhàn-zhe = standing

Move around!
dòng-yí-**dòng**
动 一 动！

You **shot** wide! No goal!
nǐ **shè** wāi le! méi jìn
你 射 歪了！没 进！
jìn = enter; wāi = bad aiming, crooked

Pass the *ball* to me.
bǎ *qiú* chuán gěi wǒ
把 球 传 给 我。

That didn't work!
bù-xíng
不 行！

Out! In! Off sides!
chū-qù! jìn-lái! biān-shàng
出 去！进来！边 上！

You have scored a goal!
nǐ **shè** zhòng le
你 射 中 了！
shè zhòng = good aiming

(*Quiet* Play)   (*ān-jìng* de yóu-xì 安 静 的 游 戏）

Play a *quiet* game and rest!
wán yī-gè *ān-jìng* de yóu-xì, rán-hòu xiū-xì
玩 一个安 静 的 游 戏，然 后 休 息。
rán-hòu = then, after; wán = have fun, play; yóu-xì = play, game; xiū-xì = rest

98

Let's **put** <u>this</u> *puzzle* <u>piece</u> in there.
bǎ <u>zhè-kuài</u> *pīn-tú* **fàng** zhè-er
把 这 块 拼 图 放 这 儿。

Which piece is <u>missing</u>?
<u>shǎo-le</u> **nǎ-kuài**
少 了 哪 块?

Do you **think** this *puzzle* <u>piece</u> goes here?
nǐ **jué-de** <u>zhè-kuài</u> *pīn-tú* shì **fàng** zhè-er ma
你 觉 得 这 块 拼 图 是 放 这 儿 吗?

<u>This piece</u> doesn't fit.
<u>zhè-kuài</u> bú-duì
这 块 不 对。
duì = correct

This **puzzle** is <u>too</u> / easy/ *hard*/.
zhè-gè **pīn-tú** <u>tài</u>/ róng-yì/ *nán*/.
这 个 拼 图 太/ 容 易/ 难/。

Look *out* the <u>window</u>!
kàn <u>chuāng-*wài*</u>
看 窗 外!

What do you <u>see</u>?
nǐ <u>kàn-jiàn</u> **shén-me** lā
你 看 见 什 么 啦?

Do you **want** to *play* toy <u>cars</u> (with me)?
nǐ **xiǎng** (hé wǒ) *wán* xiǎo-<u>qì-chē</u> ma
你 想 和 我 玩 小 汽 车 吗?
xiǎo = small, little

You can sort (**arrange**) your <u>stamp collection</u>.
nǐ néng **zhěng-lǐ** nǐ-de <u>jí-yóu</u>
你 能 整 理你 的集 邮。

99

(Trains and <u>trucks</u>**) (huǒ-chē** hé <u>kǎ-chē</u> 火 车 和 卡 车**)**

All aboard!
shàng-chē là
上 车 啦!

Tickets, <u>please</u>!
qǐng ná-chū chē-**piào**
请 拿 出 车 票!

ná-chū = show

(<u>How much money</u>) What does a **one way** trip cost?
  yí-tàng <u>duō-shǎo qián</u>
  一 趟 多 少 钱?

I'm **driving**/ *backwards*/ <u>forwards</u>/.
wǒ xiàng/ <u>qián</u>/ *hòu* / **kāi**/
我 向/ 前/ 后/ 开/.

Are you *delivering* **oil** with your **oil** truck?
  nǐ shì kāi yóu-chē *sòng-yóu* de ma
  你 是 开 油 车 送 油 的 吗?
    yóu-chē = oil truck

This is not an **oil** <u>truck</u>; it's a *cattle* <u>truck</u>.
zhè bú-shì sòng-**yóu** <u>kǎ-chē</u>, zhè-shì yùn *niú* <u>kǎ-chē</u>
这 不 是 送 油 卡 车，这 是 运 牛 卡 车。

I'm **loading** my <u>truck</u> with *sand*.
wǒ bǎ *shā-zi* **zhuāng-shàng** wǒ-de <u>kǎ-chē</u>
我 把 沙 子 装 上 我 的 卡 车。

I **like** an suv pick-up <u>truck</u>.

wǒ **xǐ-huān** suv <u>kǎ-chē</u>

我 喜 欢 SUV 卡 车。

When I have my **license**, I <u>want</u> to...

wǒ yǒu jiào-**zhào** hòu, wǒ <u>xiǎng</u>...

我 有 驾 照 后， 我 想 ......

hòu = after; jiào-zhào = driver's license

Have fun! Enjoy yourself!

hǎo-hāo wán

好 好 玩！

wán = have fun, play

The more the merrier!

yuè duō yuè hǎo
越 多 越 好!

Saturday Afternoons   xīng-qī-liù xià-wǔ 星 期 六 下 午

The opportunities for using Chinese on Saturdays are unlimited. Saturdays were made for Chinese! Chores to be done using Chinese, visits to friends using Chinese, shopping, outings, sports. The list is endless as you can see.

Can I go out and play?   **wǒ néng chū-qù wán ma**
我 能 出 去 玩 吗?

Let's **go**/ to the *movies*/ to the <u>mall</u>/.
wǒ-mén **qù**/ *diàn-yǐng-yuàn* / <u>shāng-chǎng</u>/
我 们 去/ 电 影 院/ 商 场/。
qù = go or go to

May (Julie) *come* along?
(zhù-li) **néng** *lái* ma
（茱丽）能 来 吗?

102

I'd **rather** *go* to the <u>playground</u>.
wǒ **níng kě** *qù* <u>yóu-xì-chǎng</u>
我 宁 可 去 游 戏 场。

There's a *school* <u>show</u>.
xué-xiào **yǒu** yí-gè <u>biǎo-yǎn</u>
学 校 有 一 个 表 演。

There's a/ *train / garden /* <u>show</u>.
yǒu yí-gè */huǒ-chē/ huā-huì/* <u>zhǎn-lǎn</u>
有 一 个 /火 车 /花 卉 / 展 览。

It's *more* <u>fun</u>.
gèng <u>hǎo-wán</u>。
更 好 玩。

gèng = still (even) more

There's a *car* <u>show</u> at the <u>coliseum</u>.
<u>jìng-jì-chǎng</u> yǒu yí-gè *qì-chē* <u>zhǎn-lǎn</u>
竞 技 场 有 一 个 汽 车 展 览。

There's a *puppet* **show** at the <u>library</u>.
<u>tú-shū-guǎn</u> yǒu yí-gè *mù-ǒu* **biǎo-yǎn**
图 书 馆 有 一 个 木 偶 表 演。

Are you **finished** with your <u>chores</u>?
nǐ-de <u>shì-qíng</u> **zuò wán** le ma
你 的 事 情 做 完 了 吗?

wán = finish, done

We'll **take**/ the *subway*/ the <u>bus</u>/.
wǒ-mén **zuò**/ *dì-tiě*/ <u>gōng-chē</u>/.
我 们 坐/ 地 铁/ 公 车/.

We'll **drive** the <u>car</u>.
wǒ-mén **kāi**-<u>chē</u>
我 们 开 车。

103

Can we *eat* out?
wǒ-mén **néng** zài wài-biān *chī-fàn* ma
我 们 能 在 外 边 吃 饭 吗?

I **want** to eat in a / *restaurant*/ fast food place/.
wǒ **xiǎng** zài/ *cān-guǎn*/ kuài-cān-diàn/ chī-fàn
我 想 在/ 餐 馆 / 快 餐 店/ 吃 饭。

You **have** an *appointment* at the dentist's.
nǐ **yǒu** yí-gè yá-yī *yù-yuē*
你 有 一 个 牙 医 预 约。

Your **braces** *need* to be adjusted.
nǐ-de **yá-tào** *xū-yào* tiáo-zhěng
你 的 牙 套 需 要 调 整。

No, you *aren't allowed* to dye your hair/ blond/ red/!
bù-xíng, nǐ *bù-néng* bǎ tóu-fà rǎn chéng/ huáng-sè/ hóng sè/
不 行, 你 不 能 把 头 发 染 成/ 黄 色/ 红 色/!
rǎn = dye

Get in the car! We'll *go* for a short ride.
zuò dào chē lǐ, wǒ-mén *chū-qù* dōu-dōu fēng
坐 到 车 里! 我 们 出 去 兜 兜 风。
zuò = sit; dào = arrive; lǐ = inside

Call up your *friend*, and we'll **go skateboarding**.
gěi nǐ-de *péng-yǒu* dǎ-diàn-huà, wǒ-mén **qù huá-bǎn**
给 你 的 朋 友 打 电 话, 我 们 去 滑 板。
huá-hàn-bīng = roller skating (滑 旱 冰)

104

Let's <u>listen</u> to my/ CD/ ipod/.
tīng wǒ-de/ guāng-pán/ ipod/
听 我 的/ 光 盘/ ipod/。

I would **rather** *go* <u>fishing</u>.　　　*Would* you *like* to **go** <u>fishing</u>?
wǒ **níng-kě** *qù* <u>diào-yú</u>　　　　　nǐ *xiǎng* **qù** <u>diào-yú</u> ma
我 宁 可 去 钓 鱼。　　　　你 想 去 钓 鱼 吗?

We **need** bait, *hooks* and a <u>net</u>.
wǒ-mén **xū-yào** yú-ěr, *yú-gōu* hé <u>yú-wǎng</u>
我 们 需 要 鱼 饵, 鱼 钩 和 鱼 网。

You **forgot** the <u>fishing rod</u>!　　　　I **caught** a <u>fish</u>!
nǐ **wàng-le** <u>yú-gān</u>　　　　wǒ **diào-dào** yī-tiáo <u>yú</u>
你 忘 了 鱼 杆!　　　　我 钓 到 一 条 鱼!

Can't we <u>finish building</u> the *tree house*?
wǒ-mén bǎ *shù-wū* <u>gài-hǎo</u> xíng ma
我 们 把 树 屋 盖 好 行 吗?
　　xíng = be all right

I'll **go** <u>get</u> the hammer, nails, the *saw* and boards.
wǒ **qù** <u>ná</u> chuí-zi, dīng-zi, *jù* he mù-bǎn
我 去 拿 锤 子, 钉 子, 锯 和 木 板。

Meet me in the <u>back yard</u>.
hòu-yuàn **jiàn**
后 院 见。

105

Let's **go** to the <u>attic</u>.
wǒ-mén **qù** <u>gé-lóu</u>
我 们 去 阁 楼。

Let's **read** *comic* <u>books</u>.
wǒ-mén **kàn** *màn-huà* <u>shū</u>
我 们 看 漫 画 书。

Let's **watch** the *soccer* <u>match</u> (on TV).
wǒ-mén **kàn** (diàn-shì) *zú-qiú* bǐ-sài
我 们 看 （电 视）足 球 比赛。

Let's **go** <u>swimming</u>.
wǒ-mén **qù** <u>yóu-yǒng</u>
我 们 去 游 泳。

qù = go or go to

Let's **go**/ to the <u>beach</u>/ to the <u>lake</u>/.
wǒ-mén **qù**/ hǎi-biān/ hú-biān/
我 们 去/海 边/ 湖 边/。

Let's **go** <u>water</u>-skiing.
wǒ-mén **qù** huá-<u>shuǐ</u>
我 们 去 滑 水。

Let's **go**/ to the <u>ocean</u>/ to the <u>pool</u>/.
wǒ-mén **qù** / hǎi-lǐ / yóu-yǒng-chí/
我 们 去/ 海里/ 游 泳 池/。

I'll **bring** the <u>towels</u>,
wǒ **dài** <u>máo-jīn</u>
我 带 毛 巾,

the <u>umbrella</u>, the beach <u>chair</u>, the <u>pail</u>   and the <u>shovel</u>.
sǎn,   líang-yǐ,   xiǎo-tǒng   hé chǎn-zi
伞   凉 椅,   小 桶   和 铲 子。

The **water** is <u>clear</u>.   The **sky** is <u>clear</u>.
shuǐ hěn <u>qīng</u>   **tiān-kōng** <u>qíng-liǎng</u>
水 很 清.   天 空 晴 朗。

106

Watch the birds.
kàn niǎo
看 鸟。

Keep an eye on your sister!
kān hǎo nǐ mèi-mei
看 好 你 妹 妹!

Where is the sun block?
fáng-shài-yóu zài **nǎ**
防 晒 油 在 哪?

Where are the sunglasses?
mò-jìng zài **nǎ**
墨 镜 在 哪?

Where are *lunch* and drinks?
wǔ-*fàn* hé shuǐ zài **nǎ**
午 饭 和 水 在 哪?

What a **fine** *day* for swimming!
zhēn shì yóu-yóng de **hǎo** *tiān-qì*
真 是 游 泳 的 好 天 气!

What a **beautiful** *day* for water skiing!
zhēn shì huá-shuǐ de **hǎo** *tiān-qì*
真 是 滑 水 的 好 天 气!

We don't need to rent:
wǒ-mén bú-yòng zū
我 们 不 用 租:

skis,
huá xuě bǎn
滑 雪 板,
huá xuě = to ski; bǎn = board

ski poles,
huá xuě gān
滑 雪 杆,

ski boots.
huá xuě xié
滑 雪 鞋.

We **have** our own equipment.
wǒ-mén **yǒu** zì-jǐ-de zhuāng-bèi
我 们 有 自己 的 装 备。

107

My **equipment** *needs* <u>adjusting</u>.
wǒ-de **zhuāng-bèi** *xū-yào* <u>tiáo-zhěng</u>
我 的 装 备 需 要 调 整。

The **snow** is/ too *soft*/ too <u>hard</u>/.
xuě/ tài *ruǎn* / tài <u>yìng</u>/
雪/ 太 软 / 太 硬/。

How much *(money)* is a <u>ticket</u>?
duō-shǎo *qián* yì-zhāng <u>piào</u>
多 少 钱 一 张 票?

zhāng = MW – flat, rectangular objects

Where is the <u>ticket office</u>?
<u>shòu-piào-chù</u> zài **nǎ**
售 票 处 在 哪?

Don't **go** to the <u>top of the mountain</u>.
bié dào <u>shān-dǐng</u> shàng **qù**
别 到 山 顶 上 去。

dào = up to, arrive

The **hillside** is <u>too steep</u>.
shān-pō <u>tài dǒu</u>
山 坡 太 陡.

That's dangerous!
wēi-xiǎn
危 险!

Not *too* <u>fast</u>!
bié *tài* <u>kuài</u>
别 太 快!

Are you/ **hungry**/ cold/?
nǐ / **è** / lěng/ ma
你/ 饿/ 冷 / 吗?

I am **hungry**. I am <u>cold</u>.
wǒ è le. wǒ hěn <u>lěng</u>
我 饿了。我 很 冷。

Are you <u>tired</u>?
nǐ <u>lèi</u> ma
你累吗?

Let's <u>go inside</u>,
wǒ-mén <u>jìn-qù</u>
我 们 进 去,

to rest,	to eat,	to warm up.
xīu-xì	chī-fàn	nuǎn-hé nuǎn-hé
休息，	吃饭，	暖 和 暖 和。

It's **warm** in here.
zhè-lǐ hěn **nuǎn-hé**
这 里 很 暖 和。

Let's take *some* photos!
wǒ-mén zhào *jǐ-zhāng* xiàng
我 们 照 几 张 像!

jǐ = a few; zhāng = MW – flat, rectangular objects

When are we leaving?
wǒ-mén **shěn-me shí-hòu** zǒu
我 们 什 么 时 候 走?

It's time to *go* **home.**
gāi *huí*-**jiā** le
该 回 家 了。

gāi = should, ought; huí = return

There will (certainly) be a lot of traffic.
lù-shàng (yí-dìng) yǒu hěn-duō chē
路 上 (一 定) 有 很 多 车。

lù-shàng = on the road

Don't **forget to take**/ Be sure that you have/ everything.
bié **dīu xià** dōng-xī
别 丢 下 东 西。

Did you have a good time? (play)
wán-de hǎo ma
玩 的 好 吗?

wán-de = played

I had a good time. (play)
wǒ wán-de hěn hǎo
我 玩 的 很 好。

Out of sight, out of mind　　　yǎn bú jiàn, xīn bù fán
眼 不 见， 心 不 烦

Exclamations　　　jīng-tàn jù 惊 叹 句

One word says it all when the right exclamation is used. These will become a staple in your language diet. Use often and with enthusiasm!

Wonderful! Marvelous!　　**tài hǎo le**　　太 好 了!

Okay. No *problem*! Fine by me!
xíng. méi *wên-tí*. wǒ méi yì-jiàn
行， 没 问 题. 我 没 意 见!
yì-jiàn = opinion, complain

Rubbish! Nonsense!
hú-shuō. huāng-táng
胡 说! 荒 唐!

How <u>silly</u>!
yú-chǔn
愚 蠢!

I am/ sad/ happy/.
wǒ hěn/ shāng-xīn/ gāo-xìng/
我 很/ 伤 心/ 高 兴/。

110

We are **glad** that you <u>won</u>!
wǒ-mén hěn **gāo-xìng** nǐ <u>yíng le</u>
我 们 很 高 兴 你 赢 了!

Help!   Careful!
jiù-mìng   xiǎo-xīn
救 命!   小 心!

I'm sorry. It's my <u>fault</u>.
dùi-bù-qǐ. zhè-shì wǒ-de <u>cuò</u>
对 不 起 这 是 我 的 错。

Why is it taking so <u>long</u>?
wèi-shén-me zhè-me <u>jiǔ</u>
为 什 么 这 么 久?

What a <u>surprise</u>!
tài <u>yì-wài</u> le
太 意 外 了!

Is that <u>really</u> so?
shì <u>zhēn-de</u> ma
是 真 的 吗?

Good heavens!
wǒ-de tiān nà
我 的 天 哪!

Who <u>cares</u>!
méi-rén <u>zài-hu</u>
没 人 在 乎!

I don't <u>care</u>.
wǒ bú <u>zài-hu</u>
我 不 在 乎。

It's **all** the <u>same</u> to me.
dùi wǒ **dōu** <u>yí-yàng</u>
对 我 都 一 样。

It's <u>possible</u>.
hěn <u>kě-néng</u>
很 可 能。

It doesn't matter.
méi-guān-xì
没 关 系。

I **think** you have it <u>wrong</u>.
wǒ **jué-de** nǐ suàn-<u>cuò</u> le
我 觉 得 你 算 错 了。
suàn = calculate

That's (**not**) <u>important</u>.
nà hěn (**bú**) <u>zhòng-yào</u>
那 很 (不) 重 要。

That's (**not**) concern you.
méi nǐ-de shì-er
没 你 的 事 儿。

That's (**not**) <u>important</u>.
nà hěn (**bú**) <u>zhòng-yào</u>
那 很 (不) 重 要。

111

Who <u>knows</u>!
shuí <u>zhī-dào</u>
谁 知 道 !

How <u>could</u> you not <u>know</u>?
nǐ zěn-me <u>huì</u> bù <u>zhī-dào</u>
你 怎 么 会 不 知 道?

Of course (not)!
<u>dāng-rán</u> (bù)
当 然 (不)!

Sure! Correct!
<u>kěn-dìng</u>. dùi
肯 定 ! 对 !

Matter closed!
jiě-jué le
解 决 了 !
jiě-jué le – solved

What's the matter?
zěn-me lā
怎 么 啦?
lā = question word

I hope so.
wǒ xī-wàng rú-cǐ
我 希 望 如 此 。

I <u>agree</u>.
wǒ <u>tóng-yì</u>
我 同 意 。

How <u>interesting</u>!
zhēn <u>yǒu yì-si</u>
真 有 意 思 !
yì-si = meaning

How <u>funny</u>!
zhēn <u>hǎo-xiào</u>
真 好 笑 !
zhēn = really, true

That is not <u>funny</u>!
nà bù <u>hǎo-xiào</u>
那 不 好 笑 !

Nonsense!
huāng-táng
荒 唐 !

What luck!
wàn-xìng
万 幸 !
wàn-xìng =10,000 lucks

<u>Good luck</u>!
zhù nǐ <u>hǎo yùn</u>
祝 你 好 运 !
zhù = offer good wishes

It's good <u>luck</u>!
zhè-shì <u>yùn-qì</u> hǎo
这 是 运 气 好 !

Bad <u>luck</u>!
yùn-qì bù-hǎo
运 气 不 好 !

How <u>awful</u>!
zhēn <u>zāo-gāo</u>
真 糟 糕 !
zāo-gāo = mess

How <u>unfortunate</u>!
zhēn <u>dǎo-méi</u>
真 倒 霉 !

112

It's a <u>shame</u>. What a <u>pity</u>.
kě-xī. zhēn <u>kě-xī</u>
可 惜. 真 可 惜。

That's unbelievable (<u>extraordinary</u>)!
tāi <u>jīng-rén</u> le
太 惊 人 了!

How kind! How nice!
zhēn-hǎo
真 好!
zhēn = really, true

Wonderful! Marvelous!
tài hǎo le
太 好 了!

<u>Excellent</u>! Great! Terrific!
tài <u>bàng</u> le
太 棒 了!

That would be great!
nà tài hǎo le
那 太 好 了!

That's no <u>joke</u>!
nà kě bú-shì <u>kāi-wán-xiào</u>
那 可 不 是 开 玩 笑!
kě = emphasizes tone of speaker

I think so! I think <u>not</u>!
wǒ tóng-yì. wǒ <u>bù</u> tóng-yì
我 同 意! 我 不 同 意!
tóng-yì = same meaning; agree

Is that **completely** <u>clear</u>?
dōu <u>qīng-chǔ</u> le ma
都 清 楚 了 吗?

Oh, I <u>see</u>!
Òu, wǒ <u>míng-bái</u> le
噢，我 明 白 了!
míng-bái = understand, clear

There are <u>so many</u> toys!
zhè-me duō wán-jù
这 么 多 玩 具!

Have you ever seen <u>so many</u> toys!
nǐ jiàn-guò zhè-me <u>duō</u> wan-jù ma
你 见 过 这 么 多 玩 具 吗!

Exclamations _____jīng-tàn jù 惊叹句

Don't worry!
bié dān-xīn
别 担 心!

Don't be afraid!
bié hài-pà
别 害 怕!

Calm down!
bié zháo-jí
别 着 急!

It will be all right.
bú-huì yǒu-shì de
不 会 有 事 的。
huì = can, will; yǒu-shì = problem

Here it is!
zài zhè-lǐ.
在 这 里!

There you are!
gěi-nǐ
给 你!

You're between the devil and the deep blue sea.
nǐ jìn-tuì-liǎng-nán
你 进 退 两 难。
jìn-tuì-liǎng-nán = forward, backward, both difficult

It's (not) right.
(bú) duì
（不）对。

That's not necessary.
méi-yǒu bì-yào
没 有 必 要。

You'd better not!
nǐ zuì-hǎo bié zhè-yàng
你 最 好 别 这 样!
bié zhè-yàng = not do/say so

What a mess!
luàn-qī-bā-zāo
乱 七 八 糟!

Enough of that!
gòu-le
够了!

I'm fed up! I've had it up to here! (Enough!)
wǒ fán-le. wǒ shòu-gòu-le
我 烦 了！我 受 够 了!
fán-le = lose patience; shòu = be subjected to

What's to be <u>done</u>! (What can we <u>do</u>!)
zěn-mè-<u>bàn</u>. (wǒ-mén zěn-mè-<u>bàn</u>)
怎 么 办? (我 们 怎 么 办?)

What's wrong?
zěn-mè lā
怎 么 啦?

lā = question word

That's <u>true</u>, don't you think!
nà dào shì <u>zhēn-de</u>, nǐ shuō ne
那 倒 是 真 的, 你 说 呢?

You <u>know</u>…
nǐ <u>zhī-dào</u>
你 知 道…

Yes, indeed!
què-shí
确 实!

You don't **say**! <u>Really</u>! Is that true?
nà hái yòng **shuō**. <u>zhēn-de</u> ma
那 还 用 说! 真 的 吗?

hái = still, in addition

As usual/ the <u>same</u>
hé wǎng-cháng <u>yí-yàng</u>
和 往 常 一 样。

All the <u>same</u>. Just as *before*.
lǎo-yàng-zi. hé *yǐ-qián* <u>yí-yàng</u>
老 样 子. 和 以 前 一 样。

yàng-zi = appearance

What a *sneeze*!
hǎo dà de *pēn-tì*.
好 大 的 喷 嚏!

God <u>bless</u> you!
shàng-dì <u>bǎo-yòu</u> nǐ
上 帝 保 佑 你!

What are you <u>complaining</u> about?
nǐ <u>bào-yuàn</u> *shén-me*
你 抱 怨 什 么?

Nothing is the matter.
méi shì-er
没 事 儿。

115

Exclamations _____ jīng-tàn jù 惊 叹 句

Why are you <u>crying</u>?
nǐ **wèi-shén-me** <u>kū</u>
你 为 什 么 哭?

For goodness sake!
kàn zài shàng-dì miàn shàng
看 在 上 帝 面 上!

Look!
kàn
看!

<u>Danger</u>! **Caution**!
<u>wēi-xiǎn</u>. **xiǎo-xīn**
危 险! 小 心 !

That is no laughing matter!
nà kě bú-shì kāi-wán-xiào
那 可 不 是 开 玩 笑!
kāi-wán-xiào = kidding, joking

Nobody <u>likes</u> me.
méi-yǒu rén <u>xǐ-huān</u> wǒ
没 有 人 喜 欢 我.
méi rén = nobody

You must not **say** <u>that</u>!
nǐ bù-néng <u>nà-yàng</u> **shuō**
你 不 能 那 样 说!

God forbid!
qiān-wàn bié fā-shēng
千 万 别 发 生!
fā-shēng = happen; qiān-wàn = whatever you do

<u>Why</u> on earth!
<u>wei-shén-me</u>
为 什 么!

How stupid of me!
wǒ zhēn-bèn
我 真 苯!
bèn = stupid

It's immense!
hǎo-jí-le
好 极 了!
hǎo-jí-le = extremely good

That's fine.
kě-yǐ
可 以。
kě-yǐ = can, may, fine

Me too!
wǒ yě shì
我 也 是!

What do you <u>mean</u>?
nǐ shì shén-me <u>yì-si</u>
你 是 什 么 意 思?
yì-si = meaning

What are you trying to <u>say</u>?
nǐ xiǎng <u>shuō</u> **shén-me**
你 想 说 什 么?

116

Live and let live.　　kāi-xīn wán
开　心　玩.

Birthday Party　　　　shēng-rì jù-huì　生 日 聚 会

Birthdays are one of the special times in your child's life. Birthday parties are the special notice of such times. Speaking Chinese about birthdays and birthday parties will bring a happy association to learning Chinese.

Blow out the candles!　chuī là-zhú　　吹 蜡 烛!

Happy Birthday!　　　**Would** you **like to have** a birthday *party*?
shēng-rì **kuài-lè**　　　nǐ **xiǎng yào** shēng-rì *jù-huì* ma
生 日 快 乐!　　　你 想 要 生 日 聚 会 吗?

What **would** you **like** for your birthday?
nǐ guò shēng-rì **xiǎng yào** *shén-me*
你 过 生 日 想 要 什 么?

117

Birthday Party_____shēng-rì jù-huì 生 日 聚 会

We'll **invite** your <u>friends</u>.   <u>Whom</u> do you want to **invite**?
wǒ-mén **yāo-qǐng** nǐ-de <u>péng-yǒu</u>   nǐ xiǎng **yāo-qǐng** <u>shuí</u>
我 们 邀 请 你 的 朋 友。   你 想 邀 请 谁?

Maybe we could have a <u>picnic</u>!
yě-xǔ wǒ-mén qù <u>yě-cān</u>
也 许 我 们 去 野 餐 !

At the party (<u>that day</u>) we'll *have*:
shēng-rì <u>nà-tiān</u> wǒ-mén *yǒu*
生 日 那 天 我 们 有:

ice cream, games, balloons,   hats, presents, a birthday cake.
bīng-qí-lín, yóu-xì, qì-qiú,   mào-zi, lǐ-wù, shēng-rì dàn-gāo
冰 琪 淋, 游 戏, 气 球,   帽 子, 礼 物, 生 日 蛋 糕。

We <u>could have</u> the **party** *(at place)*:
wǒ-mén <u>néng</u> *(insert place)* **jù-huì**:
我 们 能 *(insert place)* 聚 会:

at home, in a restaurant,   in the park, <u>or</u> at the beach.
zài jiā-li, zài cān-guǎn   zài gōng-yuán, <u>huò-zhě</u> zài hǎi-biān
在 家 里, 在 餐 馆,   在 公 园, 或 者 在 海 边.

Birthday Party _____ shēng-rì jù-huì 生日聚会

I want to **invite** *all* my friends!
wǒ xiǎng **yāo-qǐng** wǒ-de *suǒ-yǒu* péng-yǒu
我 想 邀 请 我 的 所 有 朋 友!

I **bought** you a birthday card and *present*.
wǒ gěi nǐ **mǎi-le** yì-zhāng shēng-rì kǎ-piàn hé *lǐ-wù*
我 给 你 买 了 一 张 生 日 卡 片 和 礼 物。

zhāng = MW – flat, rectangular object

How old are you?	I don't know.	I am **five** years old.
nǐ jǐ-suì	wǒ bù-zhī-dào	wǒ **wǔ**-suì
你几岁?	我 不 知 道。	我 五 岁。

When is your birthday?　　　　My birthday is on **May** 10.
nǐ-de shēng-rì shì nǎ-tiān　　wǒ-de shēng-rì shì **wǔ-yuè** shí-hào
你 的 生 日 是 哪 天?　　　我 的 生 日 是 五 月 十 号。
nǎ-tiān = which or what day

How many **candles** does your cake *have*?　　Let's count them!
nǐ-de dàn-gāo shàng *yǒu* jǐ-gēn **là-zhú**　　wǒ-mén shǔ-yì-shǔ
你 的 蛋 糕 上 有 几 根 蜡 烛?　　我 们 数 一 数!

Blow out the **candles**!　　**Cut** the cake!
chuī **là-zhú**　　qiē dàn-gāo
吹 蜡 烛!　　切 蛋 糕!

119

I want (**to eat**)/ chocolate/ strawberry/ vanilla / ice cream.
wǒ xiǎng **chī** / qiǎo-kè-lì/ cǎo-méi / xiāng-cǎo/ bīng-qí-lín
我 想 吃 / 巧 克 力 / 草 莓 / 香 草 / 冰 琪 淋。

Divide the **cake** into *(cut into)* eight pieces.
bǎ **dàn-gāo** *qiē chéng* bā-kuài
把 蛋 糕 切 成 八 块。

qiē chéng = cut into

Delicious!   What a great party!
hǎo-chī   zhè-ge jù-huì zhēn hǎo
好 吃!   这 个 聚 会 真 好!

Much happiness to you.   All the best. Best wishes.
(Life pleasant)   (Ten thousand things as you wish)
shēng-huó yú-kuài   wànshì rú-yì
生 活 愉 快。   万 事 如 意。

Tomorrow is another day. míng-tiān shì xīn-de yì-tiān
明 天 是 新 的 一 天。

Bedtime gāi shuì-jiào le 該 睡 觉 了

This is a fine time to read a story, book or nursery rhyme to your child in Chinese. The language he or she hears before going to sleep will linger during the night preparing for a new day filled with Chinese conversation.

Sleep well. hǎo-hāo shuì 好 好 睡。

What a <u>yawn</u>!
hǎo-dà-de <u>hā-qian</u>
好 大 的 哈 欠!

You're <u>yawning</u>.
nǐ zài <u>dǎ-hā-qian</u>
你 在 打 哈 欠。

Are you/ *tired*/ <u>sleepy</u>/?
nǐ/ *lèi*/ <u>kùn</u>/ ma
你/ 累/ 困/ 吗 ?

I'm bringing you <u>to bed</u>.
wǒ dài nǐ qù <u>shuì-jiào</u>
我 带 你 去 睡 觉。
dài = take to

Do you **want** me to bring you to bed?
nǐ **xiǎng** ràng wǒ dài nǐ qù shuì-jiào ma
你 想 让　我 带你 去　睡 觉 吗？
dài = take to

I'll read you a *story* before you go to bed.
shuì-jiào qián, wǒ géi nǐ dú yí-gè *gù-shì*
睡 觉　前，我 给 你 读 一个 故 事。
dú = read; qián = before

Go *get* your book!
qù *ná* nǐ-de shū
去拿 你 的 书！

Are you *watching* TV?
nǐ zài *kàn* diàn-shì ma
你 在 看 电 视 吗？

Take off your *clothes*.
tuō *yī-fu*
脱 衣 服。

Put on your pajamas.
chuān-shàng shuì-yī
穿　上　睡 衣。

Hang up your shirt.
bǎ chèn-yī **guà-qǐ-lái**
把 衬 衣 挂 起 来。

Clean up your *clothes*!
bǎ *yī-fu* fàng hǎo
把 衣 服 放 好！
fàng hǎo = put things in order

These **socks** *need* to be washed.
zhè-xiē **wà-zi** *gāi*-xǐ-le
这 些 袜 子 该 洗 了。
gāi = should, need

Are you ready for bed?
nǐ xiǎng shuì-jiào ma
你 想　睡 觉　吗？

I don't feel well.
wǒ bù shū-fu
我 不 舒 服.
shū-fu = comfortable

My head hurts.
wǒ **tóu**-téng
我 头 疼.

122

Say, "Good night" to daddy.
gēn bà-ba **shuō** "wǎn-ān"
跟 爸 爸 说 "晚 安."
gēn = with

Did you say your prayers?
nǐ dǎo-gào le ma
你 祷 告 了 吗?

(More and more) You're getting *heavier*!
nǐ yuè-lái-yuè *zhòng* le
你 越 来 越 重 了!

Close your eyes!
bì-shàng yǎn-jīng
闭 上 眼 睛!
bì-shàng = close (used for eyes, mouth)

Lie down.
tǎng-xià
躺 下。

Be quiet. (Don't *speak*.)
bié *shuō-huà*
别 说 话。

You **must**/ stay in bed/ *sleep*/.
nǐ **bī-xū**/ dāi zài chuáng-shàng/ *shuì-jiào*/
你 必须/ 呆 在 床 上 / 睡 觉/。

You're not in bed **yet**?
nǐ **hái** méi-yǒu shàng-chuáng ma
你 还 没 有 上 床 吗?

It's not **too early** to go to bed.
xiàn-zài shuì-jiào bú **tài-zào**
现 在 睡 觉 不 太早。

Do you **want** the *light* on?
nǐ **xiǎng** kāi-zhe *dēng* ma
你 想 开 着 灯 吗?

Mommy loves you!
mā-ma ài nǐ
妈 妈 爱 你!

/Is your **diaper**/ Are you/ <u>wet</u>?
nǐ-de **niào-bù** <u>shī</u>-le ma
你 的 尿 布 湿 了 吗?

You're teething.
nǐ zài zhǎng <u>yá</u>
你 在 长 牙.
zhǎng = grow; yá = tooth

Are you **awake**? Are you <u>sleeping</u>?
nǐ **xǐng** le ma? nǐ <u>shuì-zháo-le</u> ma
你 醒 了 吗? 你 睡 着 了 吗?

Why aren't you *asleep* <u>yet</u>?
nǐ **zěn-me** <u>hái</u> méi *shuì-zháo*
你 怎 么 还 没 睡 着?

You <u>can't fall asleep</u>?
nǐ <u>shuì-bù-zháo</u> ma
你 睡 不 着 吗?
zháo – attainment of something

Don't <u>wake</u>/ him/ her/ up.
bié jiào-<u>xǐng</u>/ tā/ tā/
别 叫 醒/他/她/。

What do you <u>want</u>, my little one?
nǐ xiǎng <u>yào</u> **shén-me**, xiǎo-bù-diǎn-er
你 想 要 什 么, 小 不 点 儿?

You **scratched** your *face* in your <u>sleep</u>.
nǐ <u>shuì-jiào</u> de shí-hòu **zhuā-pò-le** *liǎn*
你 睡 觉 的 时 候 抓 破 了 脸。
pò = break something

Don't you feel well?
nǐ bù <u>shū-fu</u> ma
你 不 舒 服 吗?
shū-fu = comfortable

Do you have a <u>tummy</u> *ache*?
nǐ <u>dù-zi</u>-*téng* ma
你 肚 子 疼 吗?

Are you <u>dizzy</u>?
nǐ <u>tóu-yūn</u> ma
你 头 晕 吗?

Do you have a / **headache**/ *toothache*/ <u>fever</u>/?
nǐ/ **tóu-téng**/ *yá-téng*/ <u>fā-shāo</u>/ ma
你/ 头 疼/ 牙 疼/发 烧/ 吗?

There are **spots** on your <u>chest</u>. (Chicken pox)
nǐ <u>xiōng-kǒu</u> yǒu **dòu-dòu** (shuǐ-dòu)
你 胸 口 有 豆 豆. (水 豆)

Your **glands** are <u>swollen</u>.
nǐ-de **biǎn-táo-xiàn** <u>zhǒng</u>-le
你的扁桃腺 肿 了。
biǎn-táo = thyroid glands

Stick out your <u>tongue</u>!
bǎ <u>shé-tou</u> **shēn chū-lái**
把 舌 头 伸 出 来!
shēn = to stretch

You have the <u>flu</u>.
nǐ dé <u>liú-gǎn</u> le
你 得 流 感 了。
dé = catch, receive

You have a <u>cold</u>.
nǐ <u>gǎn-mào</u> le
你 感 冒 了。

You're/ <u>coughing</u>/ <u>sneezing</u>./
nǐ zài/ <u>kē-sòu</u> / <u>dǎ-pēn-tì</u>/
你 在/咳 嗽/打 喷 嚏/。

I'll **take** your <u>temperature</u>.
wǒ gěi nǐ **liáng-wēn-dù**
我 给 你 量 温 度.
wēn-dù = body temperature

You'll **need** something *(medicine)* for the <u>cough</u>.
nǐ **xū-yào** chī-diǎn <u>kē-sòu-yào</u>
你 需 要 吃 点 咳 嗽 药。
chī = eat, take; yào = medicine

125

Tomorrow you'll *have to* <u>rest</u>.
nǐ **míng-tiān** *bì-xū* <u>xiū-xì</u>
你 明 天 必 须 休 息。

Does your/ **arm**/ *foot*/ <u>hurt</u>?
nǐ-de/ **gē-bo**/ *jiǎo*/ <u>téng</u>/ ma
你的/ 胳膊/ 脚/ 疼 / 吗？

Do you want a **new** <u>bandaid</u>?
nǐ xiǎng huàn yí-kuài **xīn** <u>yào-bù</u> ma
你 想 换 一 块 新 药 布 吗？

huàn = change; kuài – piece of something

Did you **sleep** <u>well</u>?
nǐ **shuì-de** <u>hǎo</u> ma
你 睡 得 好 吗？

Are you (still) tired?
nǐ (hái) lèi ma
你 (还) 累 吗？

Do you *feel* better?
nǐ *jué-de* hǎo xiē ma
你 觉 得 好 些 吗？

xiē = some

May I *sleep* over (Julie's) <u>house</u>?
wǒ **néng** zài (zhū-lì) jiā *shuì-jiào* ma
我 能 在 （茱丽） 家 睡 觉 吗？

May (Julie) *sleep* over at <u>our house</u>?
(zhū-lì) **néng** zài <u>wǒ-mén</u> jiā *shuì-jiào* ma
（茱丽） 能 在 我 们 家 睡 觉 吗？

Say your prayers.
dǎo-gào
祷 告。

<u>Sleep</u> well.
hǎo-hǎo <u>shuì</u>
好 好 睡。

Pleasant <u>dreams</u>.
zuò hǎo <u>mèng</u>
做 好 梦。

zuò = make, do

126

After Rain Comes Sunshine.

yǔ guò tiān qíng
雨 过 天 晴

Weather

tiān-qì 天 气

"Everybody talks about it." Now you and your child can talk about the weather in Chinese! Share a picture book about weather with your child, and discuss the pictures using Chinese. This could be a "school" kind of chapter if you and your child want to play school. Flash cards to make, maps to draw, temperatures to record, fun to be had!

Look at the rainbow!   kàn cǎi-hóng   看 彩 虹!

It is beautiful.
tiān-qì hěn hǎo
天 气 很 好。
tiān-qì = weather

What a splendid day!
tiān-qì zhēn hǎo/
天 气 真 好!
tiān-qì = weather; zhēn = really, true

What a splendid night!
jīn-wǎn tiān-qì zhēn hǎo
今 晚 天 气 真 好!

How the *stars* underline!
xīng-*xing* zài zhǎ-yǎn
星 星 在 眨 眼!

There are no clouds.
méi-yǒu yún-cǎi
没 有 云 彩。

It is/ **sunny**/ bright/.
tiān-qì/ **qíng-lǎng** / míng-liàng/
天 气/ 晴 朗/ 明 亮/.

The **sun is shining**.
yáng-guāng càn-làn
阳 光 灿 烂。

It is very hot *today*.
jīn-tiān hěn rè
今 天 很 热。

I'm warm. It's summer! (*now*)
wǒ hěn rè. xiàn-zài shì xià-tiān
我 很 热。现 在 是 夏 天!

We're having a heat wave.
rè-làng lái xí
热 浪 来袭。
xí = attack

It's / windy/ cloudy/.
guā-fēng/ duō-yún
刮 风 / 多 云。

There's **not** *a bit of* wind. I'm sweating.
méi-yǒu *yī-diǎn-er* fēng. wǒ zài chū-hàn
没 有 一 点 儿 风。我 在 出 汗。

It's *a bit*/ cool/ cold/.
yǒu-*diǎn-er*/ liáng/ lěng/
有 点 儿/ 凉 / 冷/。

You **need** a/ *jacket*/ sweater/.
nǐ **xū-yào** yī-jiàn/ *wài-tào*/ máo-yī/
你 需 要 一 件/ 外 套/ 毛 衣/。

It's raining cats and dogs!
xià dà-yǔ le
下 大 雨 了!
dà = big

Look at/ the *rain*/ the snow/.
kàn/ *yǔ*/ xuě/
看/ 雨/ 雪/。

128

The **street** is *full* of puddles.
mǎ-lù shàng *dōu*-shì shuǐ-wā
马 路 上 都 是 水 洼。

Take off your shoes!
bǎ nǐ-de xié *tuō*-le
把 你的 鞋 脱 了！

Your shoes are *wet*.
nǐ-de xié *shī*-le
你 的 鞋 湿 了。

What an *unpleasant* day! What *awful* weather!
tiān-qì zhēn *bù-hào*
天 气 真 不 好！

It (the weather) is *bad*.
tiān-qì *bù-hào*
天 气 不 好。

It's **only** a shower.
zhǐ-shì yī-chǎng xiǎo-yǔ
只 是 一 场 小 雨。

It's getting/ *dark*/ light/.
tiān kuài/ *hēi*/ liàng/ le
天 快/ 黑/ 亮 /了。

The **sky** is/ *dark*/ gray/ bright/.
tiān-kōng/ hěn-*hēi*/ fā huī/ míng-liàng/
天 空/ 很 黑/ 发 灰/ 明 亮/。

It's **thundering** and lightning.
dǎ-léi hé shǎn-diàn
打 雷 和 闪 电。

It's hailing!
xià bīng-báo le
下 冰 雹 了！

129

Weather _____tiān-qì 天气

What a <u>storm</u>!
hǎo-dà-de <u>léi-yǔ</u>
好 大 的 雷雨！

What <u>fog</u>!
hǎo-dà-de <u>wù</u>.
好 大的 雾！

It's <u>foggy</u>.
xià-<u>wù</u>-le
下 雾了。

Wait until the *rain* <u>stops</u>.
děng *yǔ* tíng-le
等 雨 停 了。

Look at the <u>rainbow</u>!
kàn <u>cǎi-hóng</u>
看 彩 虹！

It's a **real** <u>wintery</u> day.
zhēn-shì <u>dōng-tiān</u> le
真 是 冬 天 了。

It's **beginning** to <u>snow</u>!
kāi-shǐ xià-<u>xuě</u> le
开 始 下 雪 了！

It's <u>snowing</u>.
xià-<u>xuě</u> le
下 雪 了。

It looks like / *rain*/ <u>snow</u>/ sleet/.
hǎo-xiàng zài xià/ *yǔ*/ <u>xuě</u>/ bīng-yǔ/
好 像 在 下/雨/雪/ 冰 雨/。

Snowflakes are falling!
xuě-huā <u>piāo-piāo</u>
雪 花 飘 飘！
piāo-piāo = floating

How the <u>snow</u> *sparkles*!
bái-<u>xuě</u> *jīng-yíng*
白 雪 晶 莹！

Perhaps we can <u>build</u> a *snowman*.
yě-xǔ wǒ-mén néng <u>duī</u> *xuě-rén*
也 许 我 们 能 堆 雪 人。

Let's <u>build</u> a *snowman*.
wǒ-mén <u>duī</u> *xuě-rén*
我 们 堆 雪 人。

The/ **rain**/ <u>snow</u>/ *sleet*/ has stopped.
/**yǔ**/ <u>xuě</u>/ *bīng-yǔ*/ tíng-le
/雨/雪/ 冰 雨/ 停 了。

The <u>snow</u> is *melting.*
<u>xuě</u> zài *róng-huà*
雪 在 融 化。

The <u>snow</u> *has melted.*
<u>xuě</u> *huà-le*
雪 化 了。

Spring is <u>coming.</u>
chūn-tiān <u>lái</u>-le
春 天 来 了。

Time flies.　　　　　guāng-yīn sì jiàn
　　　　　　　　　　光　阴　似　箭

Time　　　　　　　　shí-jiān 时间

What time is it?
jǐ-diǎn le
几点 了？

　　　It is one o'clock.
　　　yī-diǎn
　　　一　点。

　　　　　It is two o'clock.
　　　　　liáng-diǎn
　　　　　两　点。

　　　　　　It is quarter after three.
　　　　　　sān-diǎn yī-kè
　　　　　　三　点　一刻。

132

It is nine thirty.
jiǔ-diǎn-bàn
九 点 半。

It is a quarter of seven.
chà yī-kè qī-diǎn
差 一 刻 七 点。

It's six twenty.
liù-diǎn èr-shí
六 点 二 十。

It is twenty of seven.
liù-diǎn sì-shí
六 点 四 十。

It is eight o'clock.
bā-diǎn
八 点。

It is nine o'clock.
jiǔ-diǎn
九 点。

It is ten after ten o'clock.
shí-diǎn shí-fēn
十 点 十 分。

It's eleven o'clock.
shí-yī-diǎn
十 一 点。

It is twelve thirty.
shí-èr-diǎn-bàn
十 二 点 半。

It is/ night/ midnight/.
yè-lǐ/ bàn-yè/
夜里/半 夜/。

It is noon.
zhōng-wǔ
中 午。

It is/ morning/ afternoon/ evening/.
shàng-wǔ/ xià-wǔ/ wǎn-shàng/
上 午/ 下 午/ 晚 上/。

It is/ early/ late/.
zǎo-le/ wǎn-le
早了/ 晚 了。

It is time to sleep.
gāi shuì-jiào le
该 睡 觉 了。

gāi = should

earlier/ later/
gèng-zǎo/ gèng-wǎn/
更 早/ 更 晚/

gèng = still, more

on time/ ahead of time/
zhǔn-shí/ tí-qián/
准 时/ 提 前/

short time/ long time
duǎn shí-jiān/ cháng shí-jiān
短 时 间/ 长 时 间

as soon as possible.
yuè kuài yuè hǎo
越 快 越 好

as late as possible
yuè wǎn yuè hǎo
越 晚 越 好。

Now!
xiàn-zài
现 在!

yesterday/ today/ tomorrow/
zuó-tiān/ jīn-tiān/ míng-tiān/
昨 天/ 今 天/ 明 天/

in the past
guò-qù
过 去

in the future
jiāng-lái
将 来

134

a day ago/ two days ago/
yī-tiān qián/ liǎng-tiān qián/
一 天 前/ 两 天 前/

this week	last week	next week
zhè xīng-qī	shàng-gè xīng-qī	xià xīng-qī
这 星 期	上 个 星 期	下 星 期

this month	last month	next month
zhè yuè	shàng-gè yuè	xià yuè
这 月	上 个 月	下 月

this year	last year	next year
jīn-nián	qù-nián	míng-nián
今 年	去 年	明 年

briefly	winter, summer, spring, autumn
duǎn-zàn	dōng-tiān, xià-tiān, chūn-tiān, qiū-tiān
短 暂	冬 天，夏 天， 春 天， 秋 天

Time and tide *wait* for no <u>man</u>.
shí-jiān bù *děng* <u>rén</u>
时 间 不 等 人。

To have a great abundance   fēng-fù
丰 富

Quantities   shù-liàng 数量

No day would be complete without numbers. From sports' scores to bedtime, children hear and absorb numbers. It is only natural to include them so your Chinese day will be complete as well.

How many are there?   yǒu duō-shǎo 有 多 少？

How old is / mommy/ *daddy*/?
/ mā-ma/ *bà-ba*/ jǐ suì
/妈 妈/爸 爸/几 岁？
jǐ = how many; suì = year (of age)

How many *fingers* do you have?   I **have** *ten* fingers.
nǐ yǒu jǐ-gēn *shǒu-zhǐ*   wǒ **yǒu** *shí*-gēn shǒu-zhǐ.
你 有 几 根 手 指？   我 有 十 根 手 指 。

There is (only) *one*.   There are (only) *four*.   There is nothing.
(zhǐ) yǒu yí-gè   (zhǐ) yǒu sì-gè   shén-me dōu méi-yǒu
只 有 一 个 。   只 有 四 个 。   什 么 都 没 有 ！

136

I have none.
wǒ yí-gè dōu méi-yǒu
我 一个 都 没 有。
dōu = all, both; méi-yǒu = have not

All the *cookies* have been eaten.
suǒ-yǒu-de *bǐng-gān* dōu chī-guān le
所 有 的 饼 干 都 吃 光 了。

Count from 3 to 10.
cóng sān **shǔ** dào shí
从 三 数 到 十。

After **15** comes *16*.
shí-wǔ hòu-biān shì *shí-liù*
十 五 后 边 是 十 六。
hòu-biān = behind, back

One and one makes two.
yī jiā yī děng-yú èr
一 加一 等 于 二。
jiā = add (on); děng-yú = equals

Four minus (less) three is one.
sì jiǎn sān děng-yú yī
四 减 三 等 于 一。

Two times one makes two.
èr chéng yī děng-yú èr
二 乘 一 等 于二。
chéng = multiply

Six divided by two makes three.
liù chú èr děng-yú sān
六 除 二 等 于 三。
chú = divide

Two, four and six are even numbers.
èr, sì, liù shì ǒu-shù
二 四 六 是 偶 数。

Three, five and seven are uneven (odd) numbers.
sān, wǔ, qī shì jī-shù
三 五 七 是 奇 数。

137

Two halves: liǎng-gè èr-fēn-zhī-yī 两个二分之一。

Fractions:　fēn shù:　分　数: fēn shù = divide numbers

a half,	a third,	a fourth,	three-fourths.
èr fēn zhī yī,	sān fēn zhī yī,	sì fēn zhī yī,	sì fēn zhī sān
二分 之 一,	三 分 之一,	四分 之一,	四 分 之 三。

fēn = divide

a little /	less/	more/		/some/	a few/
yì-diǎn-er/	gèng-shǎo/	gèng-duō		yì-xiē/	jǐ-gè
一 点 儿/	更 少/	更 多		一些/	几个

several/	many/	a lot/
jǐ-gè /	hěn-duō/	hěn-duō/
几个 /	很 多 /	很 多/

Numbers shù 数

0	líng	零	14	shí-sì	十四
1	yī	一	15	shí-wǔ	十五
2	èr	二	16	shí-liù	十六
3	sān	三	17	shí-qī	十七
4	sì	四	18	shí-bā	十八
5	wǔ	五	19	shí-jiǔ	十九
6	liù	六	20	èr-shí	二十
7	qī	七	21	èr-shí-yī	二十一
8	bā	八	22	èr-shí-èr	二十二
9	jiǔ	九	23	èr-shí-sān	二十三
10	shí	十	30	sān-shí	三十
11	shí-yī	十一	31	sān-shí-yī	三十一
12	shí-èr	十二	32	sān-shí-èr	三十二
13	shí-sān	十三	33	sān-shí-sān	三十三

138

QUANTITIES_____shù-liàng 数量

40	sì-shí	四十		90	jiǔ-shí	九十
41	sān-shí-yī	四十一		91	jiǔ-shí-yī	九十一
42	sān-shí-èr	四十二		92	jiǔ-shí-èr	九十二
43	sān-shí-sān	四十三		93	jiǔ-shí-sān	九十三
50	wǔ-shí	五十		100	yì-bǎi	一百
51	wǔ-shí-yī	五十一		101	yì-bǎi-líng-yī	一百零一
52	wǔ-shí-èr	五十二		102	yì-bǎi-líng-èr	一百零二
53	wǔ-shí-sān	五十三		103	yì-bǎi-líng-sān	一百零三
60	liù-sh	六十		200	èr-bǎi	二百
61	liù-shí-yī	六十一		201	èr-bǎi-líng-yī	二百零一
62	liù-shí-èr	六十二		202	èr-bǎi-líng-èr	二百零二
63	liù-shí-sān	六十三		203	èr-bǎi-líng-sān	二百零三
70	qī-shí	七十		300	sān-bǎi	三百
71	qī -shí-yī	七十一		301	sān-bǎi-líng-yī	三百零一
72	qī -shí-èr	七十二		302	sān-bǎi-líng-èr	三百零二
73	qī -shí-sān	七十三		303	sān-bǎi-líng-sān	三百零三
80	bā-shí	八十		400	sì-bǎi	四百
81	liù-shí-yī	八十一		401	sì-bǎi-líng-yī	四百零一
82	bā-shí-èr	八十二		402	sì-bǎi-líng-èr	四百零二
83	bā-shí-sān	八十三		403	sì-bǎi-líng-sān	四百零三

500	wǔ-bǎi 五百		900	jiǔ-bǎi 九百
501	wǔ-bǎi-líng-yī 五百零一		901	jiǔ-bǎi-líng-yī 九百零一
502	wǔ-bǎi-líng-èr 五百零二		902	jiǔ-bǎi-líng-èr 九百零二
503	wǔ-bǎi-líng-sān 五百零三		903	jiǔ-bǎi-líng-sān 九百零三
600	liù-bǎi 六百		1000	yì-qiān 一千
601	liù-bǎi-líng-yī 六百零一		2000	liǎng-qiān 两千
602	liù-bǎi-líng-èr 六百零二		3500	sān-qiān-wǔ-bǎi 三千五百
603	liù-bǎi-líng-sān 六百零三		10,000	yí-wàn 一万
700	qī-bǎi 七百		100,000	shí-wàn 十万
701	qī-bǎi-líng-yī 七百零一		1,000,000	yì-bǎi-wàn 一百万
702	qī-bǎi-líng-èr 七百零二		2,000,000	liǎng-bǎi-wàn 两百万
703	qī-bǎi-líng-sān 七百零三			
800	bā-bǎi 八百			
801	bā-bǎi-líng-yī 八百零一			
802	bā-bǎi-líng-èr 八百零二			
803	bā-bǎi-líng-sān 八百零三			

Proverbs and Prayers

Proverbs and prayers are a wonderful way to use Chinese in your every day activities. They can be committed to memory and used at a moment's notice. They are also a fine way to write some of your favorite Chinese characters on wall hangings in your own home or as gifts for others.

There is no wave without wind.
wú fēng bù qǐ làng
无 风 不 起 浪。

Friendship first, competition second.
yǒu-yí dì-yī, bǐ-sài dì-èr
友 谊 第 一,比 赛 第二。

Better to light a candle than to curse the darkness.
zǔ-zhòu hēi-àn bù-rú diǎn-liàng là-zhú
诅 咒 黑 暗 不如点 亮 蜡 烛。

Proverbs and Prayers _____gé-yán hé dǎo-gào cí
格 言 和 祷 告 词

He who asks a question is a fool for a minute;
he who does not remains a fool forever.
tí-wèn zhě shì zàn-shí de shǎ-guā; bù tí-wèn zhě
提 问 者 是 暂 时 的 傻 瓜; 不 提 问 者
yǒng-yuǎn shì shǎ-guā
永 远 是 傻 瓜。

If you are in a hurry you will never get there.
yù sù zé bù dá
欲 速 则 不 达。

Diligence is the mother of good fortune.
qín-fèn shì xìng-yùn zhī mǔ
勤 奋 是 幸 运 之 母。

A man is known by his friends.   Two wrongs do not make a right.
wù yǐ lèi jù, rén yǐ qún jù   fù fù bù wéi zhèng
物 以 类 聚，人 以 群 聚。   负 负 不 为 正。

A bird in the hand is worth two in the bush.
yī-niǎo zài shǒu shèng-yú èr-niǎo zài lín
一 鸟 在 手 胜 于 二 鸟 在 林。

Things are not always what they seem.
sì shì ér fēi
似是而非。

Proverbs and Prayers _____gé-yán hé dǎo-gào cí
格 言 和 祷 告 词

Where there is a will there is a way. (Faith will move mountains.)
yǒu zhì zhě shì jìng chéng
有 志 者 事 竞 成。

As you sow, so shall you reap.
zhòng guā dé guā, zhòng dòu dé dòu
种 瓜 得 瓜, 种 豆 得 豆。

Little pitchers have big ears.
rén xiǎo ěr ling
人 小 耳 灵。

A stitch in time saves nine.
jí shí xíng shì shì bàn gāng bèi
及 时 行 事, 事 半 功 倍。

We'll cross the bridge when we come to it.
chē dào shān qián bì yǒu lù
车 到 山 前 必 有 路。

Quotes by Mother Teresa
yǐn zì xiū-nǚ tè-lì-shā
引自 修 女 特 丽 莎

God: shàng-dì: 上 帝：
We are all pencils in the hand of God.
wǒ-mén quán shì shàng-dì shǒu zhōng de bǐ
我 们 全 是 上 帝 手 中 的 笔。

Children: **hai-zi**: 孩 子:
The child is God's gift to the family.
hái-zi shì shàng-dì gěi jiā-tíng de lǐ-wù
孩 子 是 上 帝 给 家 庭 的 礼 物。

Family: **jiā-tíng**: 家 庭:
The family that prays together stays together,
yì-qǐ dǎo-gào de jiā-tíng bú-huì fēn-kāi,
一 起 祷 告 的 家 庭 不 会 分 开,

and if they stay together they will love one another as God has
loved each one of them.
rú-guǒ bù fēn-kāi, tā-mén jiāng bǐ-cǐ xiāng-ài, yīn-wéi shàng-dì ài
měi-yī-gè rén
如 果 不 分 开, 他 们 将 彼 此 相 爱, 因 为 上 帝 爱
每 一 个 人。

And works of love are always works of peace.
yǒu ài jiù yǒu hé-píng
有 爱 就 有 和 平。

Love: **ài**: 爱 :
Love begins by taking care of the closest ones, the ones at home.
ài shǐ yú zhào-gù nǐ zuì qīn-jìn de rén, nǐ-de jiā-rén
爱 始 于 照 顾 你 最 亲 近 的 人, 你 的 家 人。

Proverbs and Prayers _____ gé-yán hé dǎo-gào cí
格 言 和 祷 告 词

Happiness: kuài-lè: 快 乐：
Let no one come to you without leaving better and happier.
ràng měi-gè lái zhǎo nǐ de rén lí-kāi shí gèng hǎo gèng kuài-lè
让 每 个 来 找 你 的 人 离 开 时 更 好 更 快 乐。

Morning Prayers: chén dǎo: 晨 祷：

Dear Lord, I give you my hands to do Your work;
qīn-ài de zhǔ, wǒ yòng wǒ-de shuāng-shǒu zuò nǐ-de gōng-zuò
亲 爱 的 主，我 用 我 的 双 手 做 你 的 工 作；

I give You my feet to go Your way;
wǒ yòng wǒ-de shuāng-jiǎo zǒu nǐ-de lù
我 用 我 的 双 脚 走 你 的 路；

I give You my eyes to see as You see;
wǒ yòng wǒ-de shuāng-yǎn xiàng nǐ nà-yàng kàn shì-jiè
我 用 我 的 双 眼 像 你 那 样 看 世 界；

I give You my tongue to speak Your words;
wǒ yòng wǒ-de shé-tóu shuō nǐ-de huà
我 用 我 的 舌 头 说 你 的 话；

I give You my mind that You may think in me;
wǒ bǎ sī-xiǎng jiāo-gěi nǐ, xiǎng nǐ suǒ xiǎng
我 把 思 想 交 给 你，想 你 所 想；

I give You my spirit that You may pray in me;
wǒ bǎ líng-hún jiāo-gěi nǐ, nǐ zài wǒ xīn-zhōng dǎo-gào
我 把 灵 魂 交 给 你，你 在 我 心 中 祷 告；

145

Proverbs and Prayers _____ gé-yán hé dǎo-gào cí

格 言 和 祷 告 词

(cont.)

Above all, I give You my heart that You may love in me –
zuì zhòng-yào de shì, wǒ bǎ xīn jiāo-gěi nǐ, ràng wǒ chōng-mǎn ài-xīn –

最 重 要 的是，我 把 心交 给 你，让 我 充 满
爱心一

love the Father and love all humankind.
ài tān-fù hé zhòng-shēng.

爱天 父 和 众 生。

I give You my whole self, Lord, that You may grow in me,
wǒ bǎ yí-què jiāo-gěi nǐ, zhǔ-a, nǐ zài-wǒ xīn-zhōng chéng-zhǎng,

我 把一 切 交 给你，主啊, 你在 我 心 中 成 长,

so that it is You who lives, works and prays in me. Amen
shēng-huó, gōng-zuò hé dǎo-gào. ā-mén

生 活， 工 作 和 祷 告。阿门。

Evening Prayers: wǎn dǎo： 晚 祷：

At the end of the day just kneel and say,
zài yī-tiān jié-shù shí, guì-xià shuō

在一 天 结 束 时，跪 下 说,

Thank You Lord for Your Love today.
zhǔ à, gǎn-xiè nǐ jīn-tiān duì wǒ-de ài

主啊, 感 谢 你 今 天 对 我 的 爱.

Prayer to Our Guardian Angel: shǒu-hù tiān-shǐ dǎo-gào:
守 护 天 使 祷 告

O, Angel of God, my guardian dear,
òu, shàng-dì de tiān-shǐ, wǒ qīn-ài de shǒu-hù shén,
哦, 上 帝的 天 使, 我 亲 爱的 守 护 神,

to whom God's love commits me here,
shī ài yú wǒ
施爱 于 我,

Ever this day/ night be at my side,
rì-yè zài wǒ shēn-biān
日夜在 我 身 边,

to light and guard, to rule and guide me. Amen.
zhào-liàng hé shǒu-hù wǒ, guǎn-lǐ hé yǐn-dǎo wǒ. ā-mén
照 亮 和 守 护 我, 管 理 和 引 导 我。阿门

Thanksgiving Prayer: gǎn-ēn dǎo-gào: 感恩祷告

God our Father, thank You for Your Love today;
shàng-dì wǒ fù, gǎn-xiè nǐ jīn-tiān duì wǒ-de ài
上 帝 我 父, 感 谢 你 今 天 对 我 的爱;

Thank You for my family and all the friends You give to me.
gǎn-xiè nǐ gěi wǒ jiā-tíng hé péng-yǒu
感 谢 你 给 我 家 庭 和 朋 友。

Guard me in the dark of night; in the morning send Your light.
zài hēi-yè zhōng shǒu-hù wǒ, zài lí-míng sòng-lái guāng-míng
在 黑 夜 中 守 护 我,在 黎 明 送 来 光 明.

147

Our Father: wǒ-fù: 我 父

Our Father Who are in Heaven,
tiān-táng wǒ-fù
天 堂 我 父,

Hallowed be Thy Name;
shén-shèng zhī míng
神 圣 之 名;

Thy Kingdom come,
wáng-guó jiàng-lín
王 国 降 临,

Thy will be done on earth as it is in Heaven;
zài rén-jiān rú-tóng zài tiān-táng
在 人 间 如 同 在 天 堂;

Give us this day our daily bread;
gěi wǒ-mén měi-rì miàn-bāo
给 我 们 每日 面 包;

And Forgive us our trespasses,
kuán-shù wǒ-mén de zuì-guò
宽 恕 我 们 的 罪 过,

As we forgive those who trespass against us.
wǒ-mén yuán-liàng nà-xiē qīn-fàn wǒ-mén de rén
我 们 原 谅 那 些 侵 犯 我 们 的 人。

And lead us not into temptation
yǐn-dǎo wǒ-mén yuǎn lí yòu-huò
引导 我 们 远 离 诱 惑,

But deliver us from evil. Amen"
jiù wǒ-mén chū mó-zhǎng. ā-mén
救 我 们 出 魔 掌。阿门

Prayers in Brief: jiǎn-duǎn dǎo-gào: 简短祷告

Thanks be to God.
gǎn-xiè shàng-dì
感 谢 上 帝

Praise You Lord
zàn-měi zhǔ
赞 美 主

Song of the Swan
tiān-é zhī gē
天 鹅之 歌

Swan, Swan, Swan,
Graceful long neck curved, singing toward the sky,
Like a white cloud floating on the jade water,
Red palms pedal the crystal clear wave.

é,   é,   é,
鹅，鹅，鹅，
qū jǐng xiàng tiàn gē,
曲 颈 向 天 歌，
bái-yún fú lǜ-shuǐ,
白 云 浮 绿 水，
hǒng-zhǎng bō qīng-bō。
红 掌 拨 清 波。

Festival

Qing Ming Festival   qìng-méng jié 清 明 节

The start of spring is signaled by the festival of Qing Ming, which falls on April 5. Many Chinese go on picnics and on trips to the countryside. They fly kites and admire the beauty of nature. Qing Ming literally means "pure brightness." On this day people also go to graves and pay their respects to their ancestors. "Jasmine Flower" is a traditional song often sung by children and women on this day.

Jasmine Flower

What a beautiful jasmine flower,
hǎo yi duǒ měi-lì de mò-lì-huā
好 一 朵 美 丽 的 茉 莉 花，
Fragrant, pretty, on the branch,
fēn-fāng měi-lì mǎn zhī-yá
芬 芳 美 丽 满 枝 桠，
White and fragrant, praised by all,
yòu-bái yòu-xiāng rén-rén kuā
又 白 又 香 人 人 夸，
Let me pick a jasmine flower,
ràng wǒ lái jiāng nǐ zhāi xià
让 我 来 将 你 摘 下，
To give to someone,
sòng gěi bié-rén jiā
送 给 别 人 家，
Jasmine flower, jasmine flower!
mò-lì-huā, mò-lì-huā
茉 莉 花，茉 莉 花！

(source: China: a portrait of the country through its festivals and traditions. Danbury, CT : Grolier Educational, 1999.)

150

Pronunciation Guide

The following information is provided to answer basic questions regarding Chinese pronunciation. This guide should be considered an approximation. It is difficult to express precise spoken sounds in written symbol.

Vowels		English Sound	Chinese Word
	a	f<u>a</u>ther	cha
a	ai	k<u>i</u>te	zai
	ao	h<u>o</u>w	hao
e	e	s<u>i</u>r	ge
	ei	h<u>ay</u>	bei
	i	s<u>ea</u>	n<u>i</u>
	i after z,c,s,zh,ch,sh & r	h<u>u</u>rry	sh<u>i</u>
i	ia	<u>ya</u>cht	x<u>ia</u>
	iao	m<u>eow</u>	<u>yao</u>
	ie	<u>ye</u>sterday	<u>ye</u>
	iu	<u>yo</u>del	<u>you</u>
o	o	s<u>ore</u>	du<u>o</u>
	ou	s<u>o</u>	d<u>ou</u>
	u	t<u>oo</u>	b<u>u</u>
	ua	<u>wa</u>nt	g<u>ua</u>
u	uo	<u>wa</u>s	<u>wo</u>
	uai	<u>wi</u>de	h<u>uai</u>
	ui	<u>wei</u>ght	sh<u>ui</u>
	ü	f<u>ew</u>	l<u>ü</u>

Vowels Plus Nasal Sound

Nasal Vowels	English Sounds	Chinese Word
a an	man	ban
ang	sang	tang
e en	thunder	men
eng	hunger	neng
i in	tin	jin
ian	yen	dian
iang	yang	jiang
ing	ringer	ling
iong	young	xiong
o ong	young	dong
u un	wonder	wen
uan	wangle	huan
uang	long wong ("ong" from "long" with a "w" in front)	huang
nü	"une" in French	nü

Consonants

b – bay	bei	p – puppy	pa	zh – jolly	zhai
c – fits	cai	q – chilly	qi	ch – chisel	chi
d – dog	da	r – raid	re	sh – shall	shi
f – full	feng	s – sad	song		
g – go	geng	t – tone	tong		
h – loch	hui	x – shrill	xia		
j – gentle	ji	z – pads	zao		
k – kitten	kai				
l – land	la				
m – my	ma				
n – no	na				

152

VOCABULARY

The Family (and Other Persons): Jiātíng 家庭

mother/ mom	mā-ma 妈妈	grandson	sūn-zi 孙子
father/ dad	bà-ba 爸爸	daughter	nǚ-ér 女儿
grandmother	nǎi-nai 奶奶	son	ér-zi 儿子
grandfather	yé-yè 爷爷	older sister	jiě-jiē 姐姐
cousin (m)	biǎo-gē/biǎo-dì 表哥/表弟	younger sister	mèi-mei 妹妹
cousin (f)	biǎo-jiě/biǎo-mèi 表姐/表妹	older brother	gē-ge 哥哥
wife	qī-zi 妻子	younger brother	dì-di 弟弟
husband	zhàng-fu 丈夫	girl	nǚ-hái-er 女孩儿
woman	nǚ-rén 女人	boy	nán-hái-er 男孩儿
man	nán-rén 男人	child	hái-zi 孩子
aunt	gū-gu/ā-yí 姑姑/阿姨		
uncle	shū-shu/bó-bo 叔叔/伯伯		
niece	zhí-nǚ 侄女	Mister	xiān-shēng 先生
nephew	zhí-zi 侄子	Missus	tài-tai 太太
grand-daughter	sūn-nǚ 孙女	Miss	xiǎo-jiě 小姐

Colors: Yán-sè 颜色

green	lǜ-sè 绿色	yellow	huáng-sè 黄色
blue	lán-sè 蓝色	purple	zi-sè 紫色
black	hēi-sè 黑色	pink	fěn-sè 粉色
white	bái-sè 白色	brown	zōng-sè 棕色
orange	jú-hóng-sè 橘 红色	gray	huī-sè 灰色
red	hóng-sè 红色	beige	huī-zōng-sè 灰棕色

Days of the Week: Xīng-qī 星期

Monday	xīng-qī yī 星期一	Friday	xīng-qī wǔ 星期五
Tuesday	xīng-qī èr 星期二	Saturday	xīng-qī liù 星期六
Wednesday	xīng-qī sān 星期三	Sunday	xīng-qī tiān 星期天
Thursday	xīng-qī sì 星期四		

Months of the Year: Yuè 月

January	yī-yuè 一月		July	qī-yuè 七月
February	èr-yuè 二月		August	bā-yuè 八月
March	sān-yuè 三月		September	jiǔ-yuè 九月
April	sì-yuè 四月		October	shí-yuè 十月
May	wǔ-yuè 五月		November	shí-yī-yuè 十一月
June	liù-yuè 六月		December	shí-èr-yuè 十二月

Seasons of the Year: Jì-jié 季节

spring	chūn-tiān 春天		autumn	qiū-tiān 秋天
summer	xià-tiān 夏天		winter	dōng-tiān 冬天

Holidays of the Year: Jié-rì 节日

Birthday	shēng-rì 生日	Mother's Day	mǔ-qīn jié 母亲节
New Year's	xīn-nián 新年	Father's Day	fù-qīn jié 父亲节
Valentine's Day	qíng-rén jié 情人节	July 4	qī-yuè sì-rì 七月四日
Passover	yú-yuè jié 逾越节	Halloween	wàn-shèng jié 万盛节
Easter	fù-huó jié 复活节	Thanksgiving Day	gǎn-ēn jié 感恩节
Christmas	shèng-dàn jié 圣诞节	Christmas Eve	--
		-- shèng-dàn qián-xī 圣诞前夕	

Nursery: Yīng-ér shì 婴儿室

bath tub	xǐ-zǎo pén 洗澡盆	night light	yè-dēng 夜灯
book	shū 书	pacifier	nǎi-zuǐ 奶嘴
bottle	nǎi-píng 奶瓶	picture	zhào-piān 照片
carriage	yīng-ér chē 婴儿车	potty	niào-pén 尿盆
crib	yīng-ér chuáng 婴儿床	rocker	yáo-lán 摇篮
diaper	niào-bù 尿布	safety pin	--
high chair	gāo-yǐ-zī 高椅子	-- ān-quán bié-zhēn 安全别针	
Mother Goose	é-mā-ma 鹅妈妈	stroller	yīng-ér chē 婴儿车
		toy	wán-jiù 玩具

155

Toys: Wán-jiù 玩具

ball	qiú 球		paint brush	huà-bǐ 画笔
balloon	qì-qiú 气球		paste	yóu-ní 油泥
bat	qiú-bàng 球棒		picture book	tú-huà shū 图画书
bead	zhū-zi 珠子		piggy bank	chǔ-xù guan 储蓄罐
bicycle	jiào-tà-chē 脚踏车		plane	fēi-jī 飞机
block	jī-mù 积木		puppet	mù-ǒu 木偶
boat	chuán 船		puzzle	pīn-tú 拼图
bull dozer	tuī-tǔ-jī 推土机		race car	caì-chē 赛车
bus	gōng-gòng-qì-chē 公共汽车		rake	pá-zi 耙子
car	qì-chē 汽车		rattle	bō-làng-gǔ 波浪鼓
chess board	chí-pán 棋盘		ring	huán 环
clay	nián-tǔ 粘土		rocket	huǒ-jiàn 火箭
clown	xiǎo-chǒu 小丑		rocking horse	yáo-mǎ 摇马
cowboy	niú-zǐ 牛仔		rope	shéng-zi 绳子
crayon	là-bǐ 蜡笔		sandbox	shā-xiāng 沙箱
doll	wá-wa 娃娃		scissors	jiǎn-dāo 剪刀
drum	gǔ 鼓		scooter	huá-xíng chē 滑行车
earring	ěr-huán 耳环		seesaw	qiào-qiào-bǎn 翘翘板
fishing rod	diào-yú gān 钓鱼杆		shovel	chǎn-zi 铲子
fort	bǎo-lěi 堡垒		skate (ice)	bīng-xié 冰鞋
game	yóu-xì 游戏		skate(roller)	huá-lún xié 滑轮鞋
globe	dì-qiú yí 地球仪		skateboard	huá-bǎn 滑板
helicopter	zhí-shēng fēi-jī 直升飞机		sled	xuě-qiào 雪橇
hoop	huán 环		slide	huá-tī 滑梯
horn	lǎ-bā 喇叭		soldier	shì-bīng 士兵
jump rope	tiào-shéng 跳绳		submarine	qiǎn-shuǐ-těng 潜水艇
kite	fēng-zhēng 风筝		swing	qiū-qiān 秋千
marble	tán-qiú 弹球		tank (military)	tǎn-kè 坦克
mask	miàn-jù 面具		teddy bear	wán-jù xióng 玩具熊
necklace	xiàng-liàn 项链		tennis racquet	wǎng-qiú pāi 网球拍
oil truck	yóu-chē 油车		tent	zhàng-péng 帐篷
paint box	huà-hé 画盒		toy box	wán-jiù xiāng 玩具箱

Toys: Wán-jiù 玩具

tow truck	tuō-chē 拖车	truck	kǎ-chē 卡车
tractor	tuō-lā-jī 拖拉机	wagon	huò-chē 货车
train	huǒ-chē 火车	wheelbarrow	dú-lún-chē 独轮车
tricycle	sān-lún-chē 三轮车	whistle	shào-zi 哨子

Clothes: Yī-fú 衣服

Backpack	bēi-bāo 背包	rubber (boot)	jiāo-xié 胶鞋
bathrobe	yù-páo 浴袍	sandal	liáng-xié 凉鞋
bathing suit	yóu-yǒng-yī 游泳衣	scarf	wéi-jīn 围巾
bathing trunks	yóu-yǒng-kù 游泳裤	shirt	chèn-yī 衬衣
belt	dài-zi 带子	shoe	xié 鞋
bib	weí-zuǐ 围嘴	shoelace	xié-dài 鞋带
blouse	chèn-shān 衬衫	shorts	duǎn-kù 短裤
boot	xuē-zi 靴子	skirt	qún-zi 裙子
cap	wú-yán-mào 无檐帽	slip	tào-qún 套裙
coat	wài-tào 外套	slipper	tuō- xié 拖鞋
dress	wài-yī 外衣	sneakers	qiú-xié 球鞋
glove	shǒu-tào 手套	snow suit	huá-xuě fú 滑雪服
handkerchief	shǒu-juàn 手绢	sock	wà-zi 袜子
hat	mào-zi 帽子	stocking	cháng-wà 长袜
jacket	jiá-kè 夹克	sweat suit	yùn-dòng yī 运动衣
jeans	niú-zǐ-kù 牛仔裤	sweater	máo-yī 毛衣
mitten	wú zhǐ shǒu-tào 无指手套	tee-shirt	hàn-shān 汗衫
nightgown	cháng shuì-yī 长睡衣	tie	lǐng-dài 领带
overcoat	dà-yī 大衣	tights	jǐn-shēn yī 紧身衣
pajamas	shuì-yī 睡衣	umbrella	yǔ-sǎn 雨伞
panties	chèn-kòu 衬裤	underpants (boys)	nèi-kù 内裤
pantyhose	kù-wà 裤袜	undershirt	nèi-yī 内衣
pants	kù-zi 裤子	underwear	nèi-yī- kù 内衣裤
pocketbook	pí-jiā 皮夹	wallet	qián-bāo 钱包
rain coat	yǔ-yī 雨衣	windbreaker	fēng-yī 风衣

Entertainments: Yú-lè 娱乐

amusement park	yóu-lè yuán 游乐园	party	jù-huì 聚会
aquarium	shuǐ-zú guǎn 水族馆	picnic	yě-cān 野餐
beach	hǎi-bīn 海滨	playground	yóu-lè chǎng 游乐场
badminton	yǔ-máo qiū 羽毛球	reading	yuè-dú 阅读
baseball	bàng-qiú 棒球	recess (school) --	
basketball	lán-qiú 篮球	-- xué-xiào fàng-jià 学校放假	
bowling	bǎo-líng-qiú 保龄球	restaurant	fàn-diàn 饭店
camping	yě-yíng 野营	rowing	huá-chuán 划船
circus	mǎ-xì 马戏	sailing	háng-hǎi 航海
concert	yīn-yuè-huì 音乐会	shopping	gòu-wù 购物
cycling	qí-chē 骑车	skating	huá-bīng 滑冰
fairground	lù-tiān shì-chǎng 露天市场	soccer	zu-qiú 足球
fishing	diào-yú 钓鱼	sports	yùn-dòng 运动
football	měi-shì zú-qiú 美式足球	stamp collecting	jí-yóu 集邮
game, match	bǐ-sài 比赛	swimming	yóu-yǒng 游泳
golf	gāo-ěr-fū-qiú 高尔夫球	tennis	wǎng-qiú 网球
gymnastics	tǐ-cāo 体操	theatre	xì-yuàn 戏院
hiking	dēng-shān 登山	volleyball	pái-qiú 排球
movie	diàn-yǐng 电影	walking	zǒu-lù 走路
movie theatre	diàn-yǐng yuàn 电影院	windsurfing	chōng-làng 冲浪
museum	bó-wù-guǎn 博物馆	zoo	dòng-wù-yuán 动物园
park	gōng-yuán 公园		

Beverages: Yǐn-liào 饮料

beer	pí-jiǔ 啤酒	orange juice	jú-zi zhī 桔子
cocoa	kě-lè 可乐	soda	qì-shuǐ 汽水
coffee	kā-fēi 咖啡	tea with lemon --	
lemonade	níng-méng-zhī 柠檬汁	-- níng-méng chá 柠檬茶	
milk	niú-nǎi 牛奶	water	shuǐ 水
		wine	jiǔ 酒

Human Body: Rén-tǐ 人体

ankle	jiǎo-wàn 脚腕		face	liǎn 脸
arm	shǒu-bì 手臂		finger	shǒu-zhǐ 手指
back	hòu-bèi 后背		finger nail	shǒu-zhǐ-jiā 手指甲
belly	dù-zi 肚子		forehead	qián-é 前额
belly button	dù-qí 肚脐		hair	tóu-fà 头发
cheek	miàn-jiá 面颊		hand	shǒu 手
chest	xiōng 胸		head	tóu 头
chin	xià-bā 下巴		heel	jiǎo-gēn 脚跟
ear	ěr-duō 耳朵		hip	tún 臀
elbow	zhǒu-bù 肘部		jaw	è 颚
eye	yǎn-jīng 眼睛		knee	xī-gài 膝盖
eyebrow	yǎn-méi 眼眉		leg	tuǐ 腿
eyelid	yǎn-pí 眼皮		lip	zuǐ-chún 嘴唇
mouth	zuǐ-bā 嘴巴		thumb	mǔ-zhǐ 拇指
neck	bó-zi 脖子		toe	jiǎo-zhǐ 脚趾
nose	bí-zi 鼻子		tongue	shé-tóu 舌头
shoulder	jiān-bǎng 肩膀		tooth	yá-chǐ 牙齿
stomach	wèi 胃		waist	yāo 腰
throat	hóu-lóng 喉咙		wrist	shǒu-wàn 手腕

Containers: Róng-qì 容器

bag	dài-zi 袋子		envelope	xìn-fēng 信封
bottle	píng-zi 瓶子		jar --	
box	hé-zi 盒子			-- guǎng-kǒu-píng 广口瓶
can	guan-tóu 罐头		top, cover	gài-zi 盖子
carton	zhǐ-hé 纸盒		tube	guǎn-zi 管子
crate	bǎn-tiáo-xiāng 板条箱		wrapper --	
				-- bāo-zhuāng wù 包装物

Dessert: Diǎn-xīn 点心

apple pie	píng-guǒ xiàn-bǐng 苹果馅饼	milk shake --	
cake	dàn-gāo 蛋糕	-- nǎi-guǒ yǐn-liào 奶果饮料	
candy	tǎng-guǒ 糖果	pancake	jiān-bǐng 煎饼
candy bar	tǎng-guǒ tiáo 糖果条	pastry	gāo-diǎn 糕点
chocolate	qiǎo-kè-lì 巧克力	pie	xiàn-bǐng 馅饼
cookie	bǐng-gān 饼干	pudding	bù-dīng 布丁
croissant	yuè-xíng diǎn-xīn 月形点心	rice pudding	mǐ-bù-dīng 米布丁
custard	nǎi-dàn-hú 奶蛋糊	sponge cake	hǎi-mián dàn-gāo 海绵蛋糕
donut	quān-bǐng 圈饼	turnover --	
gelatin	guǒ-dòng 果冻	--ban-yuán-xíng juǎn-bǐng 半圆形卷饼	
ice cream	bīng-qí-lín 冰淇淋	yoghurt	suān-nǎi 酸奶

Vegetables: Shū-cài 蔬菜

asparagus	lú-sǔn 芦笋	onion	yáng-cōng 洋葱
beet	tián-cài 甜菜	parsley	ōu-qín 欧芹
Brussel sprout	tāng-cài 汤菜	pea	wān-dòu 豌豆
cabbage	juǎn-xīn-cài 卷心菜	pepper	qīng-jiāo 青椒
carrot	hú-luó-bo 胡萝卜	potato	tǔ-dòu 土豆
cauliflower	huā-yē-cài 花椰菜	pumpkin	nán-guā 南瓜
celery	qín-cài 芹菜	radish	xiǎo-luó-bo 小萝卜
corn	yù-mǐ 玉米	spinach	bō-cài 菠菜
cucumber	huáng-guā 黄瓜	squash	guā 瓜
garlic	suàn 蒜	stringbean	dòu-jiǎo 豆角
lettuce	shēng-cài 生菜	tomato	fān-qié 番茄
mushroom	mó-gū 蘑菇	turnip	luó-bo 萝卜

Meat: Ròu 肉

bacon	xián-zhū-ròu 咸猪肉	lamb chop	yáng-pái 羊排
chicken	jī 鸡	pork chop	zhū-pái 猪排
frankfuter	xiáng-cháng 香肠	roast	kǎo 烤
ham	huǒ-tuǐ 火腿	roast beef	kǎo niú-ròu 烤牛肉
hamburger	hàn-bǎo 汉堡	sausage	xiáng-cháng 香肠
hot dog	rè-gǒu 热狗	steak	niú-pái 牛排
lamb	yáng 羊	turkey	huǒ-jī 火鸡

Seafood: Hǎi-wèi 海味

carp	lǐ-yú 鲤鱼	salmon --	
cod	xuě-yú 鳕鱼	-- dà-mǎ-hā-yú 大马哈鱼	
flounder	bǐ-mù-yù 比目鱼	sardine	shā-dīng-yú 沙丁鱼
herring	fēi-yú 鲱鱼	shrimp	xiā 虾
lobster	lóng-xiā 龙虾	trout	guī-yú 鲑鱼
		tuna	jīn-qiāng-yú 金枪鱼

Other Foods: Qí-tā shí-wù 其他食物

bread	miàn-bāo 面包	noodles	miàn-tiáo 面条
bun	xiǎo-miàn-bāo 小面包	oatmeal	yàn-mài-piàn 燕麦片
butter	huáng-yóu 黄油	pancake	jiān-bǐng 煎饼
cereal (hot)	mài-piàn 麦片	peanut	huā-hēng 花生
cheese	gān-lào 干酪	peanut butter	huā-hēng jiàng 花生酱
cornflakes	yù-mǐ-piàn 玉米片	pepper	hú-jiāo 胡椒
cracker	bǐng-gān 饼干	pickle	suān-huáng-guā 酸黄瓜
cream	nǎi-yóu 奶油	pop-corn	bào-mǐ-huā 爆米花
crumb	miàn-bāo-zhā 面包渣	potato chips	zhá-shǔ-piàn 炸薯片
egg	dàn 蛋	pumpkin	nán-guā 南瓜
(hard boiled) egg	zhǔ-dàn 煮蛋	rice	mǐ 米
flour	miàn-fěn 面粉	roll	juǎn-bǐng 卷饼
French fries	zhá-shǔ-tiáo 炸薯条	salad	shā-là 沙拉
fried eggs	chǎo-dàn 炒蛋	salt	yán 盐
gravy	ròu-zhī 肉汁	sandwich	sān-míng-zhì 三明治
honey	fēng-mì 蜂蜜	sauce	jiàng 酱
jam, jelly	guǒ-jiàng 果酱	soup	tāng 汤
ketchup	fān-qié jiàng 番茄酱	spaghetti	yì-dà-lì miàn 意大利面
mashed potatoes	tǔ-dòu ní 土豆泥	stew	dùn-cài 炖菜
mayo	dàn-huáng jiàng 蛋黄酱	sugar	táng 糖
milk chocolate --		syrup	táng-jiāng 糖浆
-- niú-nǎi qiǎo-kè-lì 牛奶巧克力		toast --	
mustard	jiè-mò 芥末	-- kǎo miàn-bāo piàn 烤面包片	
		vinegar	cù 醋

Fruits and Berries: Shuǐ-guǒ 水果

apple	píng-guǒ 苹果	lemon	níng-méng 柠檬
applesauce	píng-guǒ jiàng 苹果酱	orange	gān-jú 柑桔
apricot	xìng 杏	peach	táo 桃
banana	xiāng-jiāo 香蕉	pear	lí 梨
berry	jiāng-guǒ 浆果	pineapple	bō-luó 菠萝
blueberry	lán jiāng-guǒ 篮浆果	plum	lǐ-zi 李子
cherry	yīng-táo 樱桃	prune	gān-méi 干梅
coconut	yē-zi 椰子	raisin/s	pú-táo-gān 葡萄干
grape	pú-táo 葡萄	raspberry	fù-pén-zi 覆盆子
grapefruit	pú-táo-yù 葡萄柚	strawberry	cǎo-méi 草莓
grapes (bunch)	pú-táo chuan 葡萄串	tangerine	jú-zi 桔子
		watermelon	xī-guā 西瓜

Utensils: Chú-fáng yòng-jù 厨房用具

bottle	píng-zi 瓶子	pot	guō 锅
bowl	wǎn 碗	saucepan	zhǔ-guō 煮锅
cup	bēi-zi 杯子	saucer	xiǎo-pán-zi 小盘子
fork	chā-zi 叉子	skillet	qiǎn-guō 浅锅
glass	bō-lì-bēi 玻璃杯	soup plate	tāng-pán 汤盘
kettle	shuǐ-hú 水壶	spoon	tiáo-gēng 调羹
knife	dāo 刀	tablecloth	zhuō-bù 桌布
mug	cí-bēi 磁杯	tablespoon	tāng-chí 汤匙
napkin	cān-jīn-zhǐ 餐巾纸	teapot	chá-hú 茶壶
pitcher	shuǐ-guàn 水罐	teaspoon	chá-sháo 茶勺
plate	pán-zi 盘子	tray	tuō-pán 托盘
platter	dà qiǎn-pán 大浅盘		

Dwellings: Zhù-zhái 住宅

apartment	gōng-yù 公寓	country house	xiāng-cūn fáng 乡村房
bungalow	píng-fáng 平房	hotel	lǚ-guǎn 旅馆
cabin	xiǎo-wū 小屋	mobile home	huó-dòng fáng 活动房
condominium	gōng-yù 公寓	tent	zhàng-péng 帐篷

House: Fáng-zi 房子

attic	gé-lóu 阁楼	hallway	zǒu-láng 走廊
back door	hòu-mén 后门	hose	ruǎn-guǎn 软管
basement	dì-xià-shì 地下室	kitchen	chú-fáng 厨房
bathroom	yù-shì 浴室, cèsuǒ 厕所	lawn	cǎo-dì 草地
bedroom	wò-shì 卧室	lawn sprinkler	cǎo-dì sǎ-shuǐ-qì 草地撒水器
ceiling	tiān-huā-bǎn 天花板	living room	kè-tīng 客厅
chimney	yān-cōng 烟囱	mail box	yóu-xiāng 邮箱
dining room	cān-tīng 餐厅	roof	fáng-dǐng 房顶
door	mén 门	room	fáng-jiān 房间
fence	lí-bā 篱笆	stair	lóu-tī 楼梯
flag	qí-zi 旗子	step	tái-jiē 台阶
floor	dì-bǎn 地板	toilet	mǎ-tǒng 马桶
front door	qián-mén 前门	wall	qiáng 墙
garden	huā-yuán 花园	window	chuāng-hù 窗户
gate	lí-bā-mén 篱笆门	yard	yuàn-zi 院子

Kitchen: Chú-fáng 厨房

apron	wéi-qún 围裙	mop	tuō-bǎ 拖把
broom	sào-zhǒu 扫帚	oven	kǎo-xiāng 烤箱
cabinet	chú-guì 橱柜	pail	tǒng 桶
closet	bì-chú 壁橱	pot	guō 锅
clothes washer	xǐ-yī-jī 洗衣机	pressure cooker	gāo-yā-guō 高压锅
computer	diàn-nǎo 电脑	refrigerator	bīng-xiāng 冰箱
counter	guì-tái 柜台	sewing machine	féng-rèn-jī 缝纫机
detergent	qīng-jié-jì 清洁剂	sink	shuǐ-chí 水池
dish cloth	xǐ-wǎn-bù 洗碗布	sponge	hǎi-mián 海绵
dish washer	xǐ-wǎn-jī 洗碗机	stool	xiǎo-dèng-zi 小凳子
dust cloth	mǒ-bù 抹布	stove	lú-zi 炉子
dustpan	bò-jí 簸箕	strainer	lù-wǎng 滤网
egg beater	dǎ-dàn-qì 打蛋器	table	zhuō-zi 桌子
funnel	lòu-dǒu 漏斗	toaster --	
iron	yùn-dǒu 熨斗	-- kǎo miàn-bāo-piàn jī 烤面包片机	
ironing board	yùn-bǎn 熨板	vacuum cleaner	xī-chén-qì 吸尘器
microwave oven	wēi-bō-lú 微波炉	wax	là 蜡

163

Bathroom: Yù-shì 浴室

aspirin	ā-sī-pí-lín 阿斯匹林		perfume	xiāng-shuǐ 香水
bath towel	yù-jīn 浴巾		powder	fěn 粉
bathtub	yù-pén 浴盆		razor (electric)	(diàn-dòng) guā-hú-dāo
brush	fà-shuā 发刷			(电动) 刮胡刀
cologne	nán-yòng xiāng-shuǐ 男用香水		shampoo	xǐ-fà-yè 洗发液
comb	shū-zi 梳子		sink	shuǐ-chí 水池
face cloth	xǐ-liǎn-jīn 洗脸巾		soap	féi-zào 肥皂
face cream	miàn-shuāng 面霜		tissues	miàn-jīn-zhǐ 面巾纸
hair dryer	chuī-fēng-jī 吹风机		toilet	mǎ-tǒng 马桶
lipstick	chún-gāo 唇膏		toilet paper	shǒu-zhǐ 手纸
nail polish	zhí-jiǎ-yóu 指甲油		toothbrush	yá-shuā 牙刷
paper towel	zhǐ-jīn 纸巾		toothpaste	yá-gāo 牙膏

Bedroom: Wò-shì 卧室

armchair	fú-shǒu-yǐ 扶手椅		dresser	yī-guì 衣柜
bed	chuáng 床		lamp	tái-dēng 台灯
bedspread	chuáng-dān 床单		lampshade	tái-dēng-zhào 台灯罩
bedside table	chuáng-tóu-guì 床头柜		mattress	chuáng-diàn 床垫
blanket	tǎn-zi 毯子		mirror	jìng-zi 镜子
blinds	bǎi-yè-chuāng 百叶窗		pillow	zhěn-tóu 枕头
carpet	dì-tǎng 地毯		pillow case	zhěn-tào 枕套
CD player	guāng-pán jī 光盘机		outlet(electric)	diàn-mén 电门
chair	yǐ-zī 椅子		quilt	zhī-tǎn 织毯
clock	zhōng 钟		rocking chair	yáo-yǐ 摇椅
coat hanger	yī-jià 衣架		sheet	dān-zi 单子
curtain	chuāng-lián 窗帘		shutter	bǎi-yè-chuāng 百叶窗

Living Room: Kè-tīng 客厅

air-conditioner	kōng-tiáo 空调		desk	shū-zhuō 书桌
arm chair	diān-rén shā-fā 单人沙发		fireplace	bì-lú 壁炉
book shelf	shū-jià 书架		piano	gāng-qín 钢琴
bookcase	shū-guì 书柜		picture	zhào-piān 照片
carpet	dì-tǎn 地毯		radio	shōu-yīn-jī 收音机
couch	shā-fā 沙发		television	diàn-shì 电视

164

Tools: Gōng-jù 工具

ax	fǔ-zī 斧子	sandpaper	shā-zhǐ 砂纸
hammer	chuí-zi 锤子	saw	jù 锯
hose	ruǎn-guǎn 软管	scissors	jiǎn-zī 剪子
ladder	tī-zi 梯子	screw	luó-sī-dīng 螺丝钉
lawn mower	gē-cǎo-jī 割草机	screwdriver	luó-sī-dāo 螺丝刀
nail	dīng-zi 钉子	shovel	tiě-xiān 铁锹
nut	luó-miào 螺帽	trowel	xiǎo-chǎn-zī 小铲子
pitchfork	cháng-bǐng-chā 长柄叉	vise	lǎo-hǔ-qián 老虎钳
pliers	qián-zi 钳子	wheelbarrow	dú-lún-chē 独轮车
rake	pá-zi 耙子	wrench	huó-bān-shǒu 活扳手

The Car: Qì-chē 车

accelerator	jiā-sù-qì 加速器	mirror	jìng-zi 镜子
brakes	shā-chē 刹车	rear window	hòu-chuāng 后窗
bumper	huǎn-chōng-bǎn 缓冲板	seat	zuò-wèi 座位
dashboard	yí-biǎo-pán 仪表盘	starter	diǎn-huǒ-shuān 点火栓
door	mén 门	steering wheel	fāng-xiàng-pán 方向盘
engine	mǎ-dá 马达	sun visor	zhē-yáng-bǎn 遮阳板
glove compartment	shǒu-tào xiāng 手套箱	tire	lún-tāi 轮胎
headlight	chē-dēng 车灯	trunk	xíng-lì-xiāng 行李箱
hood	fā-dòng-jī gài 发动机盖	wheel	chē-lún 车轮
horn	lǎ-bā 喇叭	windshield	dǎng-fēng-bǎn 档风板
ignition	fā-huǒ zhuàng-zhì 发火装置	wiper	yǔ-shuā 雨刷
jack	qiān-jīn-dǐng 千斤顶		

Trees: Shù 树

apple	píng-guǒ 苹果	pear	lí 梨
birch	bái-huá 白桦	pine	sōng-shù 松树
cherry	yīng-táo 樱桃	plum	lǐ-zī 李子
fruit tree	guǒ-shù 果树	poplar	bái-yáng 白杨
hemlock	tiě-shān 铁衫	sequoia	hóng-shān 红杉
maple	fēng-shù 枫树	spruce	yún-shān 云杉
oak	xiàng-shù 橡树	willow	liǔ-shù 柳树

Insects: Kūn-chóng 昆虫

ant	mǎ-yǐ 蚂蚁	grasshopper	zhà-méng 蚱蜢
bumblebee	yě-fēng 野蜂	honey bee	mì-fēng 蜜蜂
butterfly	hú-dié 蝴蝶	lady bug	piáo-chóng 瓢虫
caterpillar	máo-máo-chóng 毛毛虫	mosquito	wén-zi 蚊子
cicada	chán 蝉	moth	é 蛾
cockroach	zhāng-láng 蟑螂	praying mantis	táng-láng 螳螂
cricket	xī-shuài 蟋蟀	spider	zhī-zhū 蜘蛛
dragonfly	qīng-tíng 蜻蜓	wasp	má-fēng 蚂蜂
flea	tiào-zǎo 跳蚤		
fly	cāng-yíng 苍蝇		

Stores: Shāng-diàn 商店

bakery	miàn-bāo diàn 面包店	fish market	yú-shì 鱼市
bank	yín-háng 银行	florist	huā-diàn 花店
barber shop	lǐ-fà diàn 理发店	furniture store	jia-jù diàn 家具店
beauty shop	měi-róng yuàn 美容院	gas station	jiā-yóu zhàn 加油站
butcher shop	ròu-diàn 肉店	grocery store	shí-pǐn diàn 食品店
cleaners	xǐ-yī diàn 洗衣店	hardware store	wǔ-jīn diàn 五金店
clothing store	fú-zhuāng diàn 服装店	jewelry store	zhū-bǎo diàn 珠宝店
dairy store	nǎi-pǐn diàn 奶品店	laundromat --	
lumber yard	mù-cái chǎng 木材场		--zì-zhù xǐ-yī diàn 自助洗衣店
deli	shú-shí diàn 熟食店	nursery (plants)	miáo-pǔ 苗圃
department store --		shoe store	xié-diàn 鞋店
	-- bǎi-huò diàn 百货店	toy store	wán-jù diàn 玩具店
drugstore	yào-diàn 药店		

Occupations: Zhí-yè 职业

astronaut	yǔ-háng-yuán 宇航员	mailman	yóu-dì-yuán 邮递员
baby sitter	zhào-kàn yīng-ér zhě 照看婴儿者		
baker	miàn-bāo shī 面包师	merchant	shāng-rén 商人
barber	lǐ-fà shī 理发师	minister	mù-shī 牧师
butcher	tú-fū 屠夫	model	mó-tè 模特
carpenter	mù-jiàng 木匠	nurse	hù-shì 护士
chauffeur	zhuān-chē sī-jī 专车司机	painter	fěn-shuā-gōng 粉刷工
cleaning lady	qīng-jié nǔ-gōng 清洁女工	pharmacist	yào-jì-shī 药剂师
cook	chú-shī 厨师	pilot	fēi-xíng-yuán 飞行员
dairy farmer	niú-nǎi chǎng zhǔ 牛奶场主	policeman	jǐng-chá 警察
dentist	yá-yī 牙医	priest	shén-fù 神父
doctor	yī-shēng 医生	race car driver	sài-chē-shǒu 赛车手
(bus) driver	gōng-chē sī-jī 公车司机	sailor	shuǐ-shǒu 水手
engineer	gōng-chéng-shī 工程师	salesman	tuī-xiāo-yuán 推销员
farmer	nóng-mín 农民	secretary	mì-shū 秘书
fireman	xiāo-fáng-yuán 消防员	taxi driver --	
garage mechanic	xiū-chē-gōng 修车工		--chū-zū-chē sī-jī 出租车司机
gardener	huā-jiàng 花匠	teacher	jiào-shī 教师
grocer	shí-pǐn shāng 食品商	usher (xì-yuàn)--	
hairdresser	lǐ-fà shī 理发师		--yǐn-wèi-yuán (戏 院) 引位员
housewife	zhǔ-fù 主妇	waiter	fú-wù-yuán 服务员
jeweler	zhū-bǎo shāng 珠宝商	waitress	nǔ fú-wù-yuán 女服务员
lawyer	lǜ-shī 律师	zoo keeper --	
librarian	tú-shū-guǎn yuán 图书馆员		--dòng-wù-yuán sì-yǎng-yuán
maid	nǔ-shì 女侍		-- 动物园饲养员

Vocabulary

Animals: Dòng-wù 动物

alligator	měi-zhōu è-yú 美洲鳄鱼		lion	shī-zi 狮子
bear	xióng 熊		llama	wú-fēng-tuó 无峰驼
bull	gōng-niú 公牛		mole	yǎn-shǔ 鼹鼠
camel	luò-tuó 骆驼		monkey	hóu-zi 猴子
cat	māo 猫		mouse	lǎo-shǔ 老鼠
chick	xiǎo-jī 小鸡		ox	shuǐ-niú 水牛
cow	niú 牛		pig	zhū 猪
crocodile	è-yú 鳄鱼		piglet	xiǎo-zhū 小猪
deer	lù 鹿		pony	xiǎo-mǎ 小马
dog	gǒu 狗		puppy	xiǎo-gǒu 小狗
donkey	lú 驴		rabbit	tù-zi 兔子
duck	yā-zi 鸭子		raccoon	huàn-xióng 浣熊
elephant	dà-xiàng 大象		rat	lǎo-shǔ 老鼠
fawn	xiǎo-lù 小鹿		reindeer	xùn-lù 驯鹿
fox	hú-lì 狐狸		rooster	gōng-jī 公鸡
French poodle --			seal	hǎi-bào 海豹
-- fǎ-guó juǎn-máo-gǒu 法国卷毛狗			sheep	mián-yáng 绵羊
frog	qīng-wā 青蛙		snake	shé 蛇
giraffe	cháng-jǐng-lù 长颈鹿		squirrel	sōng-shǔ 松鼠
goat	shān-yáng 山羊		tiger	lǎo-hǔ 老虎
gorilla	dà-xīng-xīng 大猩猩		turkey	huǒ-jī 火鸡
goose	é 鹅		turtle	wū-guī 乌龟
guinea pig	tiān-zhú-shǔ 天竺鼠		whale	jīng-yú 鲸鱼
hamster	cāng-shǔ 仓鼠		wolf	láng 狼
hippotamus	hé-mǎ 河马		worm(earth)	qiū-yǐn 蚯蚓
horse	mǎ 马		zebra	bān-mǎ 斑马
lamb	yáng 羊			
leopard	bào 豹			

168

Birds: Niǎo 鸟

blackbird	huà-méi 画眉	owl	māo-tóu-yīng 猫头鹰
bluebird	lán zhī-gēng-niǎo 蓝知更鸟	parrot	yīng-wǔ 鹦鹉
canary	jīn-sī-què 金丝雀	peacock	kǒng-què 孔雀
cardinal	běi-měi hóng-niǎo 北美红鸟	pelican	tí-hú 鹈鹕
chick	xiǎo-jī 小鸡	penguin	qǐ-é 企鹅
chicken	jī 鸡	pheasant	zhì 雉
crow	wū-yā 乌鸦	pigeon	gē-zi 鸽子
duck	yā-zi 鸭子	raven	wū-yā 乌鸦
duckling	xiǎo-yā-zi 小鸭子	robin	zhī-gēng-niǎo 知更鸟
eagle	yīng 鹰	seagull	hǎi-ōu 海鸥
goose	é 鹅	sparrow	má-què 麻雀
gosling	xiǎo-é 小鹅	stork	guàn 鹳
hummingbird	fēng-niǎo 蜂鸟	swallow	yàn-zi 燕子
lark	yún-què 云雀	swan	tiān-é 天鹅
nightingale	yè-yīng 夜莺	turkey	huǒ-jī 火鸡
ostrich	tuó-niǎo 鸵鸟	woodpecker --	
			-- zhuō-mù-niǎo 啄木鸟

Flowers: Huā 花

azalea	dù-juān-huā 杜鹃花	lily of the valley	líng-lán 铃兰
buttercup	jīn-fèng-huā 金凤花	carnation	kāng-nǎi-xīn 康乃馨
cowslip	yě-yīng-cǎo 野樱草	mimosa	hán-xiū-cǎo 含羞草
crocus	fān-hóng-huā 番红花	mum	jú-huā 菊花
daffodil	shuǐ-xiān-huā 水仙花	orchid	lán-huā 兰花
dahlia	tiān-zhú-huā 天竺花	pansy	sān-sè zǐ-luó-lán 三色紫罗兰
daisy	chú-jú 雏菊	peony	mǔ-diān 牡丹
dandelion	pú-gōng-yīng 蒲公英	petunia	lǎ-bā-huā 喇叭花
gardenia	zhī-zǐ-huā 栀子花	rhododendron	shí-nán 石楠
geranium	tiān-zhú-kuí 天竺葵	rose	méi-guì 玫瑰
iris	hú-dié-huā 蝴蝶花	sunflower	xiàng-rì-kuí 向日葵
lilac	zǐ-dīng-xiāng 紫丁香	sweet pea	wān-dòu 豌豆
lily	bǎi-hé 百合	tulip	yù-jīn-xiāng 郁金香
		violet	zǐ-luó-lán 紫罗兰

Along the Road: Lù-shàng 路上

airport	fēi-jī-chǎng 飞机场	motorcycle	jī-chē 机车
apartment building	gōng-yù lóu 公寓楼	motorscooter	jī-chē 机车
breakdown	chē-huài-le 车坏了	office building	bàn-gōng lóu 办公楼
bridge	qiáo 桥	to park	tíng-chē 停车
building	lóu-fáng 楼房	pedestrian	xíng-rén 行人
bus (school)	xiào-chē 校车	post office	yóu-jú 邮局
bus station	chē-zhàn 车站	road	dào-lù 道路
bus stop	chē-zhàn 车站	road sign	lù-biāo 路标
car qì-chē	汽车	sidewalk	rén-xíng-dào 人行道
church	jiào-táng 教堂	snowplow	chǎn-xuě ji 铲雪车
corner	jiǎo-luò 角落	snow mobile	xuě-chē 雪车
curb	lù-biān-lán 路边栏	speed limit	sù-xiàn 速限
expressway	kuài-xíng-dào 快行道	sports car	pǎo-chē 跑车
factory	gōng-chǎng 工厂	street	jiē-dào 街道
fence	lí-bā 篱笆	street light	lù-dēng 路灯
field	chǎng-dì 场地	taxi	chū-zū-chē 出租车
fire house	xiāo-fáng zhàn 消防站	tow truck	tuō-chē 拖车
fire plug	xiāo-fáng shuān 消防栓	tracks (railroad)	tiě-guǐ 铁轨
flat tire	biǎn-tāi 扁胎	traffic	jiāo-tōng 交通
hedge	shù-lí 树篱	traffic light --	
highway	gāo-sù gōng-lù 高速公路	--hóng-lù dēng 红绿灯	
hitch-hiking	dā-biàn-chē 搭便车	train	huǒ-chē 火车
house	fáng-zi 房子	train station	huǒ-chē zhàn 火车站
mail box	yóu-xiāng 邮箱	truck	kǎ-chē 卡车
traffic jam	jiāo-tōng dǔ-sāi 交通堵塞	tunnel	suí-dào 隧道
moped	jī-chē 机车	van --	
motorbike	jī-chē 机车	--jiào-huò liǎng-yòng chē 轿货两用车	

170

INDEX

A

about to – kuài yào 56
to ache – téng 124
to adjust – tiáo zhěng 104,108
(to be) afraid – hài pà 39,114
afternoon – xià wǔ 14,15,102
again – zài 14,17,54,73
agree with – tong yì 112
air – qì 96
aisle – tōng dào 80
airplane – fēi jī 82
all – dōu 31,111,113
all right – méi guān xi 58
all right – hǎo qǐ lái 51
allowance – ling yòng qián 63
allowed, may, can – néng 54,104
always – zǒng 56
animal – dòng wù 94,95
another – zài 38
any – rèn hé 58
anything – dōu 27
anyone – rén 70
appointment – yù yuē 104
arm – gē bo 34,126
to arrange – zhěng lǐ 99
to ask – wèn 48,54,68
asleep – shuì zháo 124
attic – gé lóu 106
awake – xǐng 124
to awaken – jiào xǐng 95
awful (mess) – zāo gāo 112

B

baby – wá wa 38,39
back (body) – hòu bèi 21
backwards – hòu tuì 46,88,100
backyard – hòu yuàn 105
bad – bù hǎo 50,112
bait – yú ěr 105
to bake – kǎo 61,62
baking powder – fā xiào fěn 62
balance – píng héng 86
ball – qiú 37,41,85,98
balloon – qì qiú 96,118
banana – xiāng jiāo 28
bandaid – yào bù 126
to bang – qiāo 38
barbecue – kǎo ròu jī 46
barefoot – guāng jiǎo 55
baseball – bang qiú 81,85
bat (baseball) – qiú bàng 85
bath – xǐ zǎo 21
bath tub – zǎo pén 21
bathroom – cè suǒ 19,52
battery – diàn chí 91
beach – hǎi biān 106,118
to beat – tiáo 61
beautiful – hǎo 33,38,71,107
because – yīn wéi 32,48,58
bed – chuáng 60,123,126
(to go to) bed – shuì jiào 121,122
before – yǐ qián 63,115,122

172

B

to begin – kāishǐ 130
behind – hòu biān 20
bell – líng 38
better and better – yuè lái yuè hǎo 74
bicycle – jiǎo tà chē 86
bill – zhàng dān 57
bird – niǎo 91,107
birthday – shēng rì 17,117,118,119
to bite – yǎo 20,36,42
bitter – kǔ 29
to bless – bǎo yòu 17,115
bland – dàn 29
blond – huáng sè 104
block – jī mù 37,41
blouse – chèn shān 61
to blow – chuī 83,96,117,119
blue – lán sè 87
board – bǎn zi 65
board – mù bǎn 105
board game – qí 87
boat – chuán 88
book – shū 57,76,106,122
both – dōu 84
bother – fán 44
bother – dòu 44
box – hé zi 45
braces (teeth) – yá tào 104
to brake – shā chē 87
brave – yǒng gǎn 72
bread – miàn bāo 30
to break – nòng huài 41
to break down – huài 90
breakfast – zǎo fàn 26,48
to breathe – hū xī 52
bright – míng liàng 128
to bring – dài 16,52,106
to browse – liú liǎn 80

B

to bring – ná lai 48
brother (older) – gēge 34
brother (younger) – dìdi 34,48,68
brush – shuā zì 25
to brush – shuā 25,93
bubble – pào 83
to bump – pèng 51
to burn – tàng zháo 46
bus – gōng chē 103
busy – máng 43
but – dàn shì 21
butter – huáng yóu 62
button – kòu zi 24
to buy – mǎi 63,76 – 79,119

C

cabinet – guì chú 63
cake – dàn gāo 61,118,119,120
to call (ph) – dǎ diàn huà 14,97,104
to camp – lù yíng 89,90
camper – lù yíng chē 89
can (container) – tǒng 65
can, may – kě yǐ 80,82,91,105
can – néng 16,25,30,48,53+
can't – bù néng 53,78
candle – là zhú 117,119
car – chē 66,90,99,103,104
card – kǎ piàn 119
to care – zài hu 111
careful – xiǎo xīn 29,40,47,84+
carefully – xiǎo xīn 29,40,91,92
carefully – zǐ xì 50
carriage – xiǎo chē 39, 46
carrot – hú luó bo 28
to carry – ná 58

C

C

C

cool – liáng 128
correct – dùi 112
cough – kē sòu 125
to cough – kē sòu 125
to count – shǔ 79,119
crayon – là bǐ 52,70,91
crooked – wāi 98
to cross – guò 46,47
to crow – jiào 95
crowded – jǐ 80
to cry – kū 36,37,42,116
cup – bēi 41
curl – juǎn fà 72
to cut – jiǎn xià lái 90
to cut – qiē 29,30,47,119+
cute – kě ài 72

D

daddy – bà ba 35,40,61,69
to dance – tiào wǔ 71
Danger! – wēi xiǎn 116
dangerous – wē xiǎn 65,108
dark – hēi 53,129
day – tiān 19,22,121
delicious – hǎo chī 31
to deliver – song 100
dentist – yá yī 104
dependable – kě kào 54
diaper – niào bù 23,124
dice – shǎi zī 87
difficult – nán 70,114
to dig – wā 64
dinner – wǎn fàn 27,30,31
dirt – dì shàng 84
dirty – zāng 20,44,49,55
dish – pán zi 58,60

D

to disobey – bù tīng huà 54
to divide – fēn 120
diving board – tiào shuǐ bǎn 84
dizzy – tóu yūn 125
to do – zuò 16,49,53,56,65,68+
doctor – yī shēng 39,82
dog – gǒu 42,57,94
doll – wá wa 41,93
don't – bié 20,27,30,37,41+
don't have – méi yǒu 69
door – mén 44,55
dough – miàn tuán 62
down – xià 82,93
downstairs – lóu xià 53
to drag – tuō 93
to draw – huà 71,91
to dream – zuò mèng 34
to dress – chuān yī 24,25,93
to drink – hē 29,30
to drive – kāi 89,91,100,103
to drop – diào 47
drum – gǔ 38
to dry – cā gān 21,60
dust – huī chén 61
to dust – dǎn huī 61
dust cloth – mǒ bù 61
to dye – rǎn 104

E

e-mail – diàn zǐ yóu jiàn 69
ear – ěr duō 20,35
early – zǎo 95,123,134
easy – róng yì 70,99
to eat – chī 26,27,29,48,63+
egg – jī dàn 61
elbow – zhǒu 27

175

E

F

F

H

H

I

J

K

kangaroo – dài shǒu 94
kayaking – huá dú mù zhōu 89
to keep – bǎo chí 86
to keep an eye on – dīng zhù 85
to keep an eye on – kān hǎo 107
to keep on – jì xù 86
to kick – tī 36,42
kind – hǎo 113
to kiss – qīn qīn 14
kitchen – chú fáng 54
kite – fēng zhēng 96
knee – xī gài 21
knife – dāo zi 28,47
knot – jié 25
to know – rèn shi 34 (person)
to know – zhī dào 112,115,119 (a fact)

L

lake – hú 90,106
to land – jiàng luò 82
large – dà 35,79
late – wǎn 58
to laugh – xiào 113,116
laundry – yī fu 62
lawn – cǎo dì 64
leaf – yè zi 64,65
leak (air,gas) – loù qì 96
to learn – xué huì 70
to leave– lí kāi 80,85,88
to leave, walk – zǒu 42,109
left (remaining) – shèng 28
left (adj) – zuǒ 47,86,97
lesson – kè 57,70
to let, allow – ràng 35,38,49,69+

L

Let go! – fàng shǒu 33
library – tú shū guǎn 103
license – zhí zhào 101
to lie down – tǎng xià 49,123
life boat – jiù shēng chuán 88
to lift – tái 97
light (lamp) – dēng 22,46,53,123
light – liàng 129
lightning – shǎn diàn 129
to like – xǐ huān 22,29,30,35+
(would) like – xiǎng 26,27,29+
like this –zhè yàng 91,92
to listen – tīng 33,50,54+
(a) little – yì diǎn er 21,28,29+
to live – zhù 18
living room – kè tīng 54
to load – zhuāng 100
to lock – suǒ 44
long – cháng 35,83
long (time) – jiǔ 111
to look – kàn 21,22,33,36,38+
to look like – kàn qǐ lái 25
to look for – zhǎo 14,24,80
loose – sōng 79,96
to lose – shū 88
(a) lot/ many – duō 109
loud – chǎo 60
loud – dà shēng 38
to love – ài 73,123
to lower (boat) – fang xià qù 88
to lower (vol) – guān xiǎo 56
luck – yùn qì 14,112
Good luck! – hǎo yùn 14,112
lunch – wǔ fàn 26,48,61,107

M

M

N

O

oar – jiǎng 89
ocean – hǎi 106
of course – dāng rán 112
Off sides! – biān shàng 98
oil – yóu 91,100
oil truck – yóu chē 100
okay! – méi guān xi 39
okay! – xíng 110
on – zài 20,27,33,40 +
on-line – shàng wǎng 69,93
one – yī 73,100,132
one time – yí cì 73
one way – yítàng 100
only – jiù 14
to open – kāi 44,45
orange juice – jú zi shǔi 30
Out! – chū qù 98
out – wài 99,104
outside – wài biān 53,55,83
oven – kǎo xiāng 62
overboard – luò shǔi 88
overdue – guò qī 57

P

to paddle – huá 89
pail – xiǎo tǒng 106
to paint – huà 69
pajama – shu ìyī 40,122
pants – kùzi 40
paper – zhǐ 68,92
park – gōng yuán 118
parking – ting chē 80
party – jù huì 117,118,120
to pass – chuán gěi 98
to pass – dì gěi 28

P

paste – jiàng hú 91
to paste – tiē 92
patience (lose) – fán le 114
to pay – fù 88
to pay attention – zhuān xīn 47
pebble – xiǎo shí tóu 51
pedal – tà bǎn 86
to pedal – cǎi tà bǎn 86
pen – bǐ 68
people – rén 95
perhaps – yě xǔ 78,130
to pet – pāi 42
photo – zhào piān 91
to pick – zhāi 84
to pick up – jiǎn 44
picnic – yě cān 118
picture – huà 69
picture (photo) – zhào piān 91
piece – kuài 65,99,120
pilot – jiào shǐ yuán 82
pit, seed – hú 29
to pitch (tent) – dā 90
pity – kě xī 113
(original) place – yuán chù 45
to place – fàng 130
to plant – zhòng 64
plate – pán zi 31
play – biǎo yǎn 103
to play – wán 17,37,46,52,63 +
to play (sports) – yùn dòng 72
playground – yóu xì chǎng 81,95,103
please (invite) – qǐng 18,42,43,48+
pool – yóu yǒng chí 84,106
port – gǎng kǒu 88
possible – kěn éng 111
pot – guō 63

S

S

S

strawberry – căo méi 120
street – mă lù 46,47,86,129
to stretch out – shēn 125
string beans – dòu jiăo 30
to stroll – sàn bù 39
strong – zhuàng 72
stubborn – gù zhí 51
to study – dú shū 69
stupid – bèn 116
subway – dì tiĕ 103
sugar –táng 62
to suit – shì hé 72103
summer – xià tiān 128,135
sun – tài yáng 91
sunglasses – mò jìng 107
sunny – qíng lăng 128
supermarket – chāo shì 76
Sure! – kĕn dìng 112
surprise – yì wài 111
to sweat – chū hàn 128
sweater – máo yī 128
to sweep – săo 60,66,85
sweet – tián 29
to swim – yóu yŏng 72,84,106,107
swing – qiū qiān 95,96
to swing – dàng 95
to swing (bat) – huī bàng 85
swollen – zhŏng 125

T

table – zhuō zi 27,59,60
tablecloth – zhuō bù 59
to take – ná 33
to take (want) – yào 28

T

to take (a break) – xiū xi 68
to take (one's hand) --
   --zhuā zhè shŏu 40
to take out – ná chū qù 57
to take (photo) – zhào xiàng 35,109
to take (a ride) – qù dōu fēng
to take (walk) – sàn bù 40,57
to take (turns) – lún liú lái 44
to take off (remove) – tuō 122,129
to take off (remove) – zhāi xià lái 58
to talk – tán 54
talkative – duō huà 33
tall – gāo 35
to taste – cháng 28
tea – chá 29,41
to teach – jiāo 68
teacher – lăo shī 67
to tear – sī pò 92
to tease – dòu 44
teddy bear – xiăo xióng 41
to teethe – zhăng yá 124
telephone – diàn huà 56,57
television – diàn shì 56,122
to tell – gào sù 19,49,52,55
to tell – jiào 48
to tell – shuō 50
temperature – wēn dù 125
tent – zhàng péng 89,90
thankful – găn xiè 73
Thanks – xiè xie 15,18,31
that – nà (ge) 32,35,43,47+
there – nà er 54,65
there is/ are – yŏu 28,68,84,109+
things – dōng xi 31,70,109
to think – xiăng 34

T

to think (agree) – tong yì 113
to think (feel) – jué de 80,99
to think – rèn wéi 48
this – zhè 53,54,56,65,72+
to throttle – jié liú gān 82
through – chuān guò 23,77
to throw – rēng 65,70,85
thundering – dǎ léi 129
ticket – piào 100,108
ticket office – shòu piào chù 108
to tidy(clean)up – shōu shi 70
to tie – jì 25
tight/ly – jǐn 79,96
time – shí jiān 70,134,135
time to – gāi 109
(on) time – àn shí 58
tired – lèi 108,121,126
today – jīn tiān 19,25,57,68+
toe – jiǎo zhǐ 21
together – yì qǐ 55,90
tomorrow – míng tiān 15,126
tongue – shé tóu 94,125
too – tài 21,42,53,64,99+
too much – tài duō 64,78,86
too (also) – yě 67,116
tooth – yá 20,38
toothache – yá téng 125
toothbrush – yá shuā 20
top of mountain – shān dǐng 108
to touch – pèng 41,44,46,79,98
towel – máo jīn 21,106
toy – wán jù 36,52,80
train – huǒ chē 100,103
trash – fèi wù 70
tree – shù 65,84
triangle – sān jiǎo 91

T

to trip – bàn dǎo 45
trouble – má fán 44
truck – kǎ chē 100,101
true – zhēn 115
truth – shí huà 50
to try – jìn liàng 85
to try – shì 29,55,79,86+
tub – zǎo pén 21
tummy – dù zi 35,73,124
turn – lún dào 57
turn – lún liú 44
to turn – zhuǎn 40,86
to turn off – guān 20,53,56
to turn on – kāi 20,53

U

umbrella – sǎn 106
unbelievable – jīng rén 113
uncle – shū shu 69
to understand – míng bái 50,73,113
underwear – nèi yī 25
upstairs – lóu shàng 53
to go upstairs – shàng lóu 48,53
unfortunate – dǎo-méi 112
to use – yòng 28,55,91+

V

to vacuum – xī chén 60,66
vacuum cleaner – xī chén qì 60
vanilla – xiāng cǎo 120
very – fēi cháng 73
to visit – kàn 37
voice – shēng yīn 71

W

wagon – xiǎo chē 65,84
to wait for – děng 43,46,54
to waken – jiào xǐng 124
to walk – sàn bù 57
to walk – zǒu lù 38,71
wall – qiáng 46
to want – xiǎng 26,35,49,58,61+
to want – yào 28,77
warm – nuǎn hé 109
warm – rè 128
to warm up – nuǎn hé 109
to wash – xǐ 20,60,66,122+
waste basket – fèi zhǐ lǒu 70
to watch – kàn 56,66,106,107,122
to watch out for – xiǎo xīn 40,64
Watch out! – xiǎo xīn 64
water – shuǐ 20,21,106
to water the flowers – jiāo huā 64
water lily – hé yè 94
water skiing – huá shuǐ 89,106,107
to wear – chuān 24,25
weather – tiān qì 127,129
weed – zá cǎo 64
to weed – chú cǎo 64
week – xīng qī 83
welcome – huān yíng 18
wet – shī 124
Well done! – hěn bàng 73
what – shén me 16,18,25,32,34,+
when – shén me shí hòu 26,109
where – nǎ 24,39,95,107+
where – nǎ er 35,37,49,67+
where – na lǐ 18,51
while – shí hòu 68
who – shuí 34,38,57,118
whose – shuí de 87

W

why – wèi shén me 30,48,60,116+
why not – wèi shén me bù 60
will – huì 16,40,45,51+
to win – yíng 88
wind – fēng 96,128
window – chuāng hù 45,99
windy – guā fēng 128
to wipe – cā 52,55
to wish – zhù 14
with – gēn 52,75
wonderful – hěn bàng 72
Wonderful! – tài hǎo le 111,113
wood – mù tóu 65
word – huà 50,54,71
work – shì er 60
to work – gàn huó er 69
to work – zuò 83
to worry – dān xīn 114
would (like) – xiǎng 26,27,63+
to wrap – bāo 63
to write – xiě 46,72
wrong – cuò 24,87,111

XYZ

yard – yuàn zi 65,81,83,85,105
yawn – hā qiàn 121
to yawn – dǎ hā qiàn 121
year – nián 17
yellow – huáng 91
yesterday – zuó tiān 67,134
yet, still – hái 123,126
You're welcome – bú xiè 18
your – nǐ de 20,24,28,34,41+
yourself – zì jǐ 24,27,30,53,73+
to zipper – lā shàng 24

Also by Therese Slevin Pirz

Kids Stuff series: Language Helper series:

Kids Stuff German   **Language Helper German**
Kids Stuff French
Kids Stuff Italian
Kids Stuff Spanish   **Language Helper Spanish**
Kids Stuff Russian   **Language Helper Russian**
Kids Stuff Inglés   **Language Helper Inglés**
Kids Stuff Angliiski   **Language Helper Angliiski**
(English)   **(English)**
Kids Stuff Chinese
Kids Stuff Yingyu (English) 2008

ABC's of SAT's:
How One Student Scored 800 on the Verbal SAT

Retirement: The How-to Book c.2011 Illustrated: 150 pp
ISBN 978-0-9789152-7-8 $29.95

You've been waiting years to retire. You want to get it right! Help is available to maneuver the twists and turns of the retirement process. Should you ~ Retire? Move? Stay local? Get another job? Downsize? Schedule? These and other questions on every retiree's mind are presented in

Retirement: The How-to Book

Save money, time and stress by avoiding costly errors in retirement preparation. There is much to learn, but this book keeps the information clear and simple.

* * * * * * * *

I wish we had read <u>Retirement: The How-to Book</u> before we started our search.   ~ Many retirees ~

§§§§§§§§§§§§§§§§§§§§§§§§§§§§§§§§§§§§

READING GUIDANCE

ABC's of SAT's: How One Student Scored 800 on the Verbal SAT
c. 2000 Illustrated; 146 pp   ISBN#: 0-9606140-9-5
Ages: *Birth to 12 years*   Grades: Pre-school to middle school $18.95

An *annotated* list of hundreds of books starting with pre-natal readings and concluding with titles for 13-year olds. This is not only the collective readings of a *Merit Scholar* who aced the verbal SAT with a perfect score of 800, but a list of books children will love and enjoy for their own merit. A list of exciting, enjoyable books, and a pain-free preparation for test-taking! A perfect combination.